TRAINING TEENAGERS FOR *Peer Ministry*

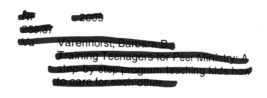

TRAINING TEENAGERS FOR *Peer Ministry*

By Dr. Barbara B. Varenhorst
With Lee Sparks

Loveland, Colorado

Training Teenagers for Peer Ministry

Designed by Judy Atwood

Scripture quotations are from the Holy Bible, New International Version. Copyright © 1973, 1978, 1984 International Bible Society. Used by permission of Zondervan Bible Publishers.

ISBN 0931-529-23-9

Printed in the United States of America

CONTENTS

Author's Note

Barbara dedicates this project to the following people:

My husband Vern, who has been my peer minister through support and sacrifice.

Pamela and James Toole, who have been my collaborators and friends for much of the program's development.

Editor's Note

Lee acknowledges and thanks the people who contributed their time and effort to this project: Renetta Backman, Lane Eskew, Jim Elsner, Walt Marcum, Les Stroh, Rich Bimler and my colleagues at Group Publishing.

*I*ntroduction

This book will not start peer ministry among your young people. They already talk with and listen to each other about their problems. Few teenagers go to adults first when they need help. This is normal and acceptable. They go first to their friends because friends are first priority in their lives. Although parents influence their teenagers, peers' influence is increasingly more important. Youth ministry is ultimately peer ministry.

But there are problems with untrained kids giving counsel to their peers. Kids often lack adequate skills for helping others effectively. Kids struggling with their identity ("Who am I?") at times feel insecure about how to find friendship and give support. They often make mistakes and act cruelly. Their developing communication skills sometimes cause miscommunication. With the purest motives, they can easily give harmful counseling.

Young people hunger to know how to love themselves so they can give love, respect and worth to the primary people in their world—their peers. I hear repeatedly from kids, "I go to my friends for help with my problems." With the more honest ones I hear, "But I don't know how to help my friends when they come to me." This program guides young people toward better self-esteem so they can reach out to friends in love, respect and caring. If we can provide this guidance, many of the problems and tragedies affecting young people can be prevented.

PURPOSES OF PEER MINISTRY

Adults often point to the negative effects of peer influence: substance abuse, self-defeating attitudes, delinquent behavior and so on. But peers can also influence each other in positive ways: teamwork, a listening ear, holding each other accountable, giving perspective, sharing Christian faith and so on.

This peer ministry training program equips young people with life skills to become the friends they would like to have. This book helps you guide, motivate and teach young people how to minister to peers in Christian love and service. Jesus gave us clear instructions for growing in our faith. The greatest commandment is to love our neighbors as ourselves. Peer ministry training helps kids grow by learning how to put the greatest commandment to work in their lives.

Another purpose of peer ministry training is to develop young people as leaders in youth ministry. Youth workers often see leadership training solely as teaching young people tasks such as how to lead meetings and Bible studies, plan retreats and edit newsletters. But peer ministry helps kids develop an often overlooked skill: *caring for those whom they lead*. And it takes courage for kids (even the leader types) to reach out to the lonely, isolated or socially handicapped. They need training. Peer ministry training will equip them with valuable skills they will need in the leadership positions they will hold as adults.

SETTINGS FOR PEER MINISTRY

Any group of teenagers in the church who truly want to learn how to be better friends to others should use this program. Peer ministry is for students who know what it's like to have problems and are willing to receive training in order to help others.

It is best that the kids *volunteer* for the training and commit some of their valuable free time to it. The ideal setting is a week night that doesn't clash with other youth ministry activities. Peer ministry training is meant as a special supplement to, not a competitor of, regular youth ministry efforts.

The training can be done in youth group or Sunday school settings. But these settings present some built-in obstacles, the greatest ones being kids who might not want to be there. Kids attending against their will might turn their attitudes around once they start the training. But if they don't, their presence will seriously affect the training experience for everyone. Their presence will negate a central theme in peer ministry: We care because we have experienced God's care and now want to share what we've received.

Each session lasts 90 minutes, but the curriculum is adaptable to 60 or 120 minutes. The ideal group will contain no fewer than eight people and no more than 20. This encourages intimacy among the members and nurtures an environment of openness and acceptance.

The program includes eight sessions of "basic" peer ministry training. Young people will learn the vital skills of listening, questioning, reading non-verbal communication, welcoming a stranger into a group, decision-making and values, sharing their faith and so on.

The program also includes six "advanced" sessions for groups that want more in-depth training. The advanced sessions also help students to apply the skills from the basic training to real-life problems of hurting peers.

THE LEADER'S ROLE

This program is only as effective as the leader who uses it. Careful thought and almost 20 years of experience in peer counseling training have been poured into these sessions. Since groups and settings vary, however, you must prepare efficiently before each session for the training to succeed. Read each session carefully. Plan how the activities will be introduced, carried out and debriefed. You will stretch your skills in group dynamics with peer ministry training. This program deals with deep emotional and spiritual needs. Prepare yourself and feed yourself, for much will be demanded of you.

Each lesson includes questions to generate discussion. These questions occur in a logical sequence. They stimulate and draw out students' thoughts and feelings. As group members begin to share, their comments and thoughts will encourage further sharing and illustrate the learning you want them to accomplish.

THE STUDENTS' ROLES

Peer ministry training depends heavily on the training group's motivation to learn. Fortunately, friendship concerns dominate teenagers' priorities. Peer ministry training requires students to involve themselves fully in the learning activities. The purpose of these activities is to provide a safe "laboratory" for students to practice the skills before they encounter real-life peer ministry counseling situations.

The learning activities will succeed if you explain clearly *what* students need to do. *How well* they perform the learning activities is their responsibility. Sometimes the students will shine as they practice the skills. Sometimes, however, they will perform an activity poorly. Yet through their failures they often learn the most. When they experience the negative effects of what can happen in counseling, they will be better prepared for the real thing.

*T*HE FORMAT OF THE SESSIONS

Let's take a brief look at the common elements of the sessions:

Session Objectives. These are the goals of the session—what students will learn.

Scripture Foundation. This highlights some of the biblical rationale for the session. The scripture and the commentary following it will give you a sense of the session's spiritual direction.

Preparation. None of the sessions requires you to gather a lot of material beforehand. Rather, this section prepares you mentally and spiritually for the session.

Opening. The opening activities warm up the students to the session. The openings get them personally involved. You can use what they share to teach the skills in the session.

Skills Development. This is the "meat" of the session. Each student will participate in learning and practicing the peer ministry skills.

Response. Debriefing and "putting it all together" is the purpose of this section. Students must connect the learning activities to real life. The discussion questions and response devices help students understand the session's learning activities.

Closing. This articulates some of the Christian implications of peer ministry skills. The Closing is devotional, intended to help students express their faith and connect it to peer ministry action.

Homework Assignment. "Faith without deeds is dead," wrote James. The Homework Assignment amplifies the skills training as students put their faith into action. I've found that students learn peer ministry skills much more quickly when they apply them and then report their experiences. Their excitement grows as they experience success in helping others.

Handouts. This section has handouts if they are needed. You have permission to photocopy, for local church use only, whatever handouts you need from this book.

Most adults who have trained students in peer ministry have found it a stimulating and meaningful experience. I trust and pray that you also will enjoy rewarding experiences. As leader, if you genuinely believe in young people and trust and encourage them, you can become a vital and important person in their lives. Their trust is a sacred privilege. This privilege demands the best from all of us who accept this responsibility and opportunity.

A WORD ABOUT THIS PROGRAM

This peer ministry program evolved from my work with peer counseling programs in public schools. In the fall of 1969, I interviewed many students in the Palo Alto, California, school district to identify some of the needs to address in an expanded guidance program. Then came the idea to teach adolescents how to help each other more effectively. The teenagers had a great desire to help friends but most lacked the skills to do so. With the help of many people, the Palo Alto Peer Counseling Program was launched in 1970. For nearly 20 years this program has been continued, expanded and adopted by schools, churches and social agencies throughout America.

In 1978, after eight years of refining the curriculum for the program, the first edition of the *Curriculum Guide for Student Peer Counseling Training* was published. A new edition was published in 1982, the same year when Les Stroh, assistant executive secretary of the Board for Youth Services of the Lutheran Church—Missouri Synod, approached me about introducing the program as "peer ministry" for the synod. To do this, *A Theological Perspective for Peer Ministry* was developed to supplement the earlier work. The idea of integrating the two works was suggested by Lee Sparks, of Group Publishing, in order to provide a single guide for youth workers to train young people in peer ministry.

The One-to-One Relationship

SESSION OBJECTIVES

Students will:
1. Meet members of the training group.
2. Show genuine interest in others.
3. Handle nervousness in conversations.
4. Initiate a conversation effectively.
5. Deal with silences in conversations.
6. Develop an awareness of the emotional "wounds" of others.
7. Develop an awareness of the negative and positive power of names and labels.
8. Develop an awareness of how self-consciousness and insecurity interfere in making friends and being a friend.
9. Talk in pairs for a 10-minute period.
10. Discuss confidentiality.
11. Explore the parable of the good Samaritan.

SCRIPTURE FOUNDATION

The Parable of the Good Samaritan

On one occasion an expert in the law stood up to test Jesus. "Teacher," he asked, "what must I do to inherit eternal life?"

"What is written in the Law?" he replied. "How do you read it?"

He answered: ' "Love the Lord your God with all

your heart and with all your soul and with all your strength and with all your mind'; and, 'Love your neighbor as yourself.' "

"You have answered correctly," Jesus replied. "Do this and you will live."

But he wanted to justify himself, so he asked Jesus, "And who is my neighbor?"

In reply Jesus said: "A man was going down from Jerusalem to Jericho, when he fell into the hands of robbers. They stripped him of his clothes, beat him and went away, leaving him half dead. A priest happened to be going down the same road, and when he saw the man, he passed by on the other side. So too, a Levite, when he came to the place and saw him, passed by on the other side. But a Samaritan, as he traveled, came where the man was; and when he saw him, he took pity on him. He went to him and bandaged his wounds, pouring on oil and wine. Then he put the man on his own donkey, took him to an inn and took care of him. The next day he took out two silver coins and gave them to the innkeeper. 'Look after him,' he said, 'and when I return, I will reimburse you for any extra expense you may have.'

"Which of these three do you think was a neighbor to the man who fell into the hands of robbers?"

The expert in the law replied, "The one who had mercy on him."

Jesus told him, "Go and do likewise."

—*Luke 10:25-37*

The body of Christ must not defer its ministry to the work of the pastoral office. The members of the body have more contact with more people and more opportunities to minister than any pastor will ever have. The church meets the needs of people and brings glory to God only in proportion to the willingness of its various members to minister. One aspect of ministry is the one-to-one relationship so powerfully illustrated in Jesus' parable of the good Samaritan.

This parable moves us beyond the tendency to hide

God's love within ourselves. If we love God, we will love our neighbor too (1 John 4:20). P.A. Sorokin describes five dimensions of love:

1. Intensity—Where is my love in the range between indifference and a willingness to give my life?

2. Extensity—How wide and inclusive is my circle of concern?

3. Duration—How long does my affection last?

4. Purity—Is my love unmixed with motives of greed or the desire to dominate?

5. Adequacy—Does my love bring to those for whom I care enrichment and fulfillment?

Peer ministry is a test of students' love. In this course, participants will gain an awareness of their neighbors and their needs. Furthermore, students will learn skills to minister in such a way that emotional and social wounds may be healed. Such awareness of others and a willingness to respond are results of Christ's love and a desire to express that love.

The story is told about the little girl who didn't want to be left alone when she was put to bed. "You've got your doll," said her mother. "Your doll will keep you company."

"When I'm lonely," the child replied, "a doll is no good to me. I want someone with skin on her face."

We all do. God comes to us in our loneliness. God gives us the opportunity to experience and express his love in one-to-one relationships with other people. The Christian has a special opportunity to reach out to the lonely, distressed and wounded. God reveals his love to others through each of us.

PREPARATION

1. Prepare the meeting area for the training group: warm, comfortable and not too large or too small. Obtain a chalkboard or newsprint pad. Photocopy a

"Guidelines for Starting Conversations" handout for each person.

2. Read carefully through the session, becoming fully prepared and aware of its objectives and learning activities.

3. To help you think through the purpose and direction of this session, answer the following questions either in writing or in thought:

● Why is it difficult for me to start conversations with strangers?

● What habits do I have that reveal my nervousness?

● If I am uncomfortable with silences, why? How do I handle this?

● Are there certain types of people or age groups who are hard for me to converse with? Explain.

● What do I need to do to improve my confidence in social situations?

● What additional questions, points or examples can I use in making this lesson meaningful?

● Additional notes to myself:

Peer Ministry Training

OPENING

1. Pray. Open with a prayer by asking for God's guidance as participants seek to serve him.

2. Introduce the purpose of peer ministry. Ask students, "Why are you taking this course?" Suggest possible reasons that they might be afraid to say. For

example: "Because my friends wanted to take it."
"My mother made me." "I wanted to learn how to
help others." Give them a short time to think before
asking for volunteers. Not many may be willing to
share, but after a few do, move on to the introduction.

Say: "This course will teach you how to reach out
to others, give friendship and help those in need. You
will learn to be more aware of others' problems and
discover specific ways you can help them. You will
learn how to listen, make friends, start conversations
and welcome others into your groups. You will discuss family, friendship and health problems and how
to help someone who suffers from the death of a
loved one or the loss of a friend. You will also explore how to share your faith with friends and how
to get help from adults when you discover problems
too serious for you to handle.

"All of this is called the 'education of the heart' because in order for you to do these things and to give
this kind of help, you need to learn to want to care
and perhaps learn new attitudes and values that affect
how you feel about yourself and how you treat others."

Cover any housekeeping duties at this time. You
may want to provide snacks for the first session and
then get volunteers to provide them at subsequent
sessions.

3. What's in a name? One of the first ways to
show interest in others is to remember their names
and how to pronounce them. To help the group
members do this for one another, ask each person to
state his or her first, middle and last name. Then talk
about these names. How do students feel about the
names they were given? Do they know why they
were given the names? What nicknames have they
had? What funny or embarrassing experiences have
they had with their names? What nationality are they?

You should *always* go first, modeling different

things that could be said about a name. When finished, tell the group what they should call you by—your first name, Mr., Mrs., etc.

Choose the first student to start. When this student has finished, have him or her choose the next person, rather than go around the circle. Not knowing when they will be chosen helps group members to listen to the "stories" each person shares about his or her name. A typical example of what you or a student might say is the following:

"My name is Ingrid Kristin Bakkun. My first name was for my grandmother who died a year before I was born and my middle name was for my father's mother. I've never liked my first name because it sounds so stiff and formal, and in elementary school people called me 'Grid,' which I hated. So when I got to junior high I started going by Kris and signing my papers just Kris Bakkun. My parents started calling me Kristy, which I liked, but when my mother gets angry she calls me Ingrid. Although now that I'm an adult I sign my checks I. Kristin Bakkun, I still go by my middle name, but don't like to be called Kristy—it sounds too juvenile. I'm Norwegian and have learned quite a lot about my heritage. Next summer I'm going to Norway to look up some of my relatives. In this class I would like you to call me Kris."

If students seem shy or brief in talking about their names, ask questions that will help them elaborate: "Have you asked your parents why they gave you the name you have?" "What is the significance of your middle name?" "What are your brothers' and sisters' names?" Encourage students to ask their parents how they got their names and to report back to the class in the next session.

Skills Development

4. Introduce confidentiality. In talking about his or her name, each person has shared something personal. This is a good opportunity to introduce confidentiality. Stress that peer ministry will never succeed if peer ministers can't be trusted to keep a confidence. This means that anything shared of a personal nature with another is not theirs to give away in gossip or idle talk. If someone in the group has shared a name he or she doesn't like, or a name he or she has tried to keep hidden, use this as an example of what you mean by confidentiality. Telling *anyone* outside the group this information, unless given permission by the person who shared it, would violate the confidentiality code.

5. Introduce the skill of observation. In most of the sessions one or two students will be asked to be an Observer of the learning activities to provide practice in "listening with their eyes." This is an important skill to learn for two primary reasons:

● Non-verbal communication often carries more significant information than verbal communication. Because non-verbal messages are spontaneous, and not as often consciously screened as are words, they may convey more honest or accurate messages. In one way or another the body always responds to what is in the mind. The more skilled one gets in observing body reactions, the more clearly one understands what a person is feeling or trying to express.

● Everyone observes constantly, either consciously or unconsciously. Interpretations are processed based on what is seen, leading to assumptions about the person or event. Actions or responses result from these assumptions, often before first checking their accuracy.

This process of observing, interpreting and checking the accuracy of interpretation and responding constitutes total listening to what another person is saying. This enhances interpersonal relationships. The following diagram illustrates this process:

Observe ▶ Interpret ▶ Check ▶ Respond = Total Listening

In introducing this listening skill, you should include the reason for learning it; how it is helpful to being an effective peer counselor; and the method for practicing it. Demonstrate this skill by acting as the Observer for this session. Allow individuals to react to your observations at the end of the session.

6. The power of names. As students talked about their names, they might have expressed subsequent feelings that affect their self-concept or behavior. For example: "Ingrid made me feel too old or stiff." "Kristy made me feel too juvenile." "David is a biblical name and I find I want to live up to the name." These comments illustrate the power of names.

If you have time, briefly explain the significance of names throughout the Bible. Names changed when a person's character or behavior changed. Saul changed his name to Paul after his conversion. Ask a volunteer to read John 1:35-42 to the class. Jesus looked at Peter and said in verse 42: "You are Simon son of John. You will be called Cephas" (that is, Peter, meaning "a rock"). Through this, Jesus was teaching us the importance of our names. Jesus valued Peter, not only for what he was, but for what he could become. Long before he was regarded as a man of rock, Jesus gave him a name that would always remind him of the Master's faith in him. So it is with ourselves. Our names have meaning in terms of the people we are, and who we are becoming.

Likewise, the names we give to others carry power. When family members or close friends use names that are intimate and loving, we feel wanted and special. But when we use names or labels that are ugly, unkind or judgmental, we make others feel dirty, dumb, worthless or unacceptable. These negative names sometimes stay imprinted in people's self-concepts. Ask the following questions:

● What names have you used or have heard used that are intended to hurt or put down another person?

● Why do we use negative or derogatory names or labels in contacts with others?

● How does it make you feel when you are called such names?

● How does it make you feel when you use such names or labels?

● How much effort would it take to refrain from using them?

● How might refraining from using such names or labels contribute to helping others? How might it affect your school's atmosphere? your youth group's?

7. Let's get better acquainted. Ask students to pick a partner, one whom they don't know, or whom they know the least. If possible, have them pick a partner of the opposite sex.

Tell the pairs they can go anywhere in the room and they will have 10 minutes to get to know each other. Although this may seem painful or difficult for some to continue the conversation for this length of time, stick to the 10 minutes. Some may get up and leave their partners or just sit and say nothing. But all of these reactions can be used later to teach the purposes of the lesson. If students finish conversations early, observe what they do before you gather the group together for the Response.

After 10 minutes, call the group back together in a circle.

RESPONSE

Use the following questions for debriefing this activity and helping students respond to what they have experienced. Questions under the "Necessary transition questions" section should always be asked. The points you want to emphasize are summarized following the questions.

8. Necessary transition questions:

● How did you feel when I said to choose someone you didn't know?

● How did you choose your partner?

● What were the reasons why you chose who you did?

● What did you think about when you were looking for a partner for this exercise?

9. Examining the experience:

● What opening topics or questions did you use to get started?

● How successful were they?

● What were you worried about as you began your conversation?

● What feelings did you pick up that your partner was feeling?

● How did you handle any nervousness?

● How did you handle any silences?

● What did you do to help your partner feel more comfortable?

● What was the balance in sharing in the conversation? Was one person more dominant?

● How did your partner communicate interest in you?

● What was most meaningful to you about this experience?

● What makes it hard to meet a new person outside of class?

● What kinds of social situations seem most

uncomfortable to you?

● How could others help you feel more comfortable in these situations?

● What is one thing you can do to help others feel comfortable?

● When was the last time you initiated a conversation with a new student in your school or with someone whom you felt was lonely? Why would you avoid this? What might you gain in making the effort?

● Review with the whole group the "Guidelines for Starting Conversations" handout. If the 10-minute exercise went poorly, ask students to repeat it after reviewing the guidelines.

10. Points to make about the learning activity:

● Initial questions about how it felt to choose a partner are critical. Push for an expression of students' *feelings*. Feelings reveal a variety of insecurities that prevent people from reaching out to others. As participants discuss their feelings, they realize that their fears are not unique. Rather, almost everyone feels this way.

● Illustrate that those who were chosen to be a partner were honored. Often we hold back from initiating a contact because we are afraid the person won't want to talk to us, or we won't know what to say. This self-consciousness restrains us from reaching out. Actually, when one approaches another out of genuine interest, the recipient is honored.

● There are a variety of ways to show we are truly interested in another. We demonstrate this in the types of questions asked, picking up on something the other has said and following through with in-depth questions about the subject. Facial expressions, tone of voice and body postures also indicate our interest in the person we are getting to know.

● It's important to recognize when people are nervous and how to respond in caring ways. The shy person often is silent, causing the other to get nervous or to withdraw. When we realize *why* a person is silent, we may be more creative in developing the conversation.

● The most effective way to initiate one-to-one relationships is being genuinely interested in getting to know the other person and conveying a warmth and acceptance. If this attitude is present, then your words or body language will usually follow. Sincerity conveyed through the eyes, through listening and through honest responses will communicate care.

Because genuine interest is a critical and foundational skill, review with students the "Guidelines for Starting Conversations." Encourage students to learn these guidelines so that they will be prepared in their daily opportunities to start conversations.

CLOSING

11. Peer ministers—good Samaritans for today's hurting people. Say: "Most of us have heard or sung the phrase 'What a friend we have in Jesus.' But if we think about it, isn't it more accurate to say, 'What a *Jesus* we have in a friend'? Our goal in peer ministry is to help others the way Jesus did, one to one. Let's read a familiar story and listen carefully to how it shows peer ministry in action."

Choose a good reader to read Luke 10:25-37 aloud. After the reading, ask:

● What did the Samaritan risk in providing this help?

● What did he gain for himself in providing this help?

● What keeps you from helping or reaching out to others who are hurt socially or emotionally?

Summarize the discussion by describing the points that form the framework for peer ministry:

● Those "expected" to show mercy passed by on the other side. It was the most unlikely person who showed mercy and kindness to the wounded traveler. Even though you may feel wounded, lonely or reject-ed, you may be the very one who is needed to give help. The good Samaritan may have suffered before in some way and was helped, and therefore knew the importance of giving such help to another.

● The Samaritan had to come close and touch the wounded man to realize the extent of his need. We cannot help another from a distance or even recognize the full need of another without becoming involved.

● The Samaritan took action that involved the ex-penditure of time, energy and money. We can voice concern about another, but our true concern is revealed when we do things for others that may involve risks or sacrifices.

● Our real care is shown if we do this without any appreciation or reward, including public recognition of our acts.

Say to the group: "The question was, 'Who is my neighbor?' Peer ministry serves our neighbor, whether he or she is unlovely, ungrateful or an outsider. It is a service to those who are wounded emotionally and/or socially. In this course we will learn to become aware of those in need and learn how to minister to them in such a way that wounds may be healed. Such awareness of others and willingness to respond are results of the love of Christ and a desire to express that love."

12. Affirmation and closing prayer. Ask students to stand next to their partners, as the large group gathers in a circle. Join hands and pray aloud, all participants thanking God for something they learned today about their partners.

*H*OMEWORK ASSIGNMENT . . .

Ask each student to practice starting a conversation with a stranger such as a student in the lunchroom, a store clerk or a bus driver.

Also ask students to keep a journal of the names or labels they hear at school, including the names and labels they find themselves using.

HANDOUT:

Guidelines for Starting Conversations

1. Introduce yourself first, if this is the first meeting.

2. Open conversation with a topic that may be of interest to both of you, or with a non-threatening question, or by talking together about an object, a piece of jewelry or the clothing the other has on.

3. Ask informational questions that will provide "free information" on which the conversation may be built. Informational questions may lead to a subject of interest to both of you. For example: "Have you lived in other places?" "Have you traveled outside the country?" "Where did you go on vacation?"

4. Look at the person, making eye contact, while not doing something else at the same time.

5. Show you are listening by following a comment with a further question or comment relating to what the person just said.

6. Return comments about yourself without the other person having to ask. Avoid an interview type of situation, and develop a sharing relationship.

7. Avoid asking questions that result in either a yes or no answer.

8. Smile occasionally, but don't always laugh or giggle.

9. Use questions and a tone of voice that convey sincerity and do not sound phony.

10. Do not probe into personal areas that the speaker has not volunteered.

11. Allow silences to occur when the other person is considering what to answer, or when both of you are thinking of new directions to take the conversation.

Conversational Skills: Questioning

SESSION OBJECTIVES

Students will:

1. Help others share their interests, even if the topics are unfamiliar.

2. Identify and use different types of questions for different purposes.

3. Use questions effectively in establishing a conversational relationship.

4. Participate in a group-questioning of one group member.

5. Interview and be interviewed in a paired situation on personal interests.

SCRIPTURE FOUNDATION

What Do You Want Me to Do for You?

As Jesus approached Jericho, a blind man was sitting by the roadside begging. When he heard the crowd going by, he asked what was happening. They told him, "Jesus of Nazareth is passing by."

He called out, "Jesus, Son of David, have mercy on me!"

Those who led the way rebuked him and told him to be quiet, but he shouted all the more, "Son of David, have mercy on me!"

> *Jesus stopped and ordered the man to be brought*
> *to him. When he came near, Jesus asked him, "What*
> *do you want me to do for you?"*
> *"Lord, I want to see," he replied.*
> *Jesus said to him, "Receive your sight; your faith*
> *has healed you." Immediately he received his sight*
> *and followed Jesus, praising God. When all the peo-*
> *ple saw it, they also praised God.*
>
> —*Luke 18:35-43*

J.F. McFadyen once said a teacher should always be an animated question mark. So should a peer minister. Socrates was one of the world's greatest teachers. He was probably the world's most famous questioner. Through his questions he was able to lead people to understand principles, ideas and themselves. Jesus taught through questions also. Jesus often taught through parables, and each story invited a question. At the end of his parables always came the question, spoken or implied, "Well, what do *you* think?"

Although we have few examples of Jesus attempting to know a person better through open-ended questions, it is important to realize the power of his questions. By examining the impact of these questions, students can come to realize the strength that effective questions bring to relationships.

In Luke 18:41 Jesus asks the blind man, "What do you want *me* to do for you?" His open-ended question allows him to discover a lot about the individual.

Pilate asked Jesus during his trial, "Are you the king of the Jews?" (John 18:33-34).

Jesus responded with another question, "Is that your own idea, or did others talk to you about me?" Jesus' question demonstrated his passion for the truth and his hatred of insincerity. This is what this session implies. Questions must be sincere. They should relate to what is real in the person to whom one is talking.

*P*REPARATION

1. Prepare the meeting area for the training group: warm, comfortable and not too large or too small. Obtain a chalkboard or newsprint pad.

2. Read carefully through the session, becoming fully prepared and aware of its objectives and learning activities.

3. To help you think through the purpose and direction of this session, answer the following questions either in writing or in thought:

● What kinds of questions do I ask my husband or wife or children?

● What do I usually do when I am "caught" in a situation with a stranger? Do I say anything? Do I only ask informational questions? Do I do all of the talking to relieve the awkwardness of the situation?

● How do I handle social situations in large groups? Do I start conversations? What kinds of questions do I use to do this?

● What additional questions, points or examples can I use in making this lesson meaningful?

● Additional notes to myself:

Peer Ministry Training

*O*PENING

1. Pray. Open with a prayer by asking for God's guidance as participants seek to serve him.

2. Assign an Observer; and ask for homework reports.

3. Introduce the purpose of asking questions in conversations. Frequently young people feel they can't carry a conversation because they don't know how to find the "bridge" that connects them with the other person. Peer ministers must be skilled in knowing how to do this because the kinds of students they will work with frequently lack the skills to find those common bonds.

In introducing the purpose of this session, emphasize that knowing when and how to use effective questioning skills is only *one* part of conversations. You are not suggesting that peer ministers go around interviewing people; but knowing how to ask different types of questions helps establish warm conversations. Although this session focuses on open-ended and personal questions, frequently people have to start a conversation with some informational questions.

4. Share some information on personal interests. Ask students to think of their interests, such as a hobby, activity or subject they're studying that really gives them pleasure and enjoyment. Ask them to choose two of their most unusual interests that others might not know about them. Tell them that they will be asked to share their name and their interests. Give them time to think, then call on one and go around the circle.

After everyone has shared, choose a person who has the most unusual interest. Ask the person if he or she would let the group ask questions about his or her interest.

Ask the group members to brainstorm questions they could ask this person about this interest, without the person answering at this time. Write the questions on the board exactly as asked. When the group begins to slow down, say to the person: "Although you might like to answer all the questions on the board, indicate only the ones you would prefer to answer. When you're finished, rank the top three you would like to answer."

Now ask the students if they see any difference between the preferred and less preferred questions. The group members will probably discover that the person chose questions about personal feelings or achievements.

Ask the person to answer the top-ranked question. Then ask the group if there are more questions they could ask of the person based on the answer given to the top-ranked question. Usually there are additional ones.

Describe the four types of questions that people use in conversations:

● Closed questions—Do you like to cook? How long have you been cooking?

● Open-ended questions—What is it that you like about cooking? What was your most unusual experience with foods?

● Informational questions—When did you move to California?

● Feeling-level questions—How do you feel about living in California in contrast with Minnesota?

The opening activity illustrates that people prefer open-ended questions and feeling-level questions more than closed and informational questions. Most people are programmed to ask the informational and closed questions, which only provide answers with specific responses. But by using open-ended questions and feeling-level questions, the questioner helps others say what they want to say and provide more information for developing a conversation.

SKILLS DEVELOPMENT

5. Practice questions. Divide group members into pairs. Tell them to share for 10 minutes. One partner is interviewed about a personal interest. After five minutes the partners change roles. Emphasize that this is *not* to be a conversation but a practice in asking questions, primarily open-ended ones. This is a *questioning* exercise. After five minutes, have the pairs switch roles.

RESPONSE

Use the following questions for debriefing this activity and helping students respond to what they have experienced. Questions under the "Necessary transition questions" section should always be asked. The points you want to emphasize are summarized following the questions.

6. Necessary transition questions:
- Which role was the hardest to do?
- What made it hard?
- What made it difficult to stay in the questioning role?
- How many were trying to ask open-ended questions?

7. Examining the experience:
- What clues showed you that your questioner was interested in you?
- What kinds of questions were the most effective in helping you get to know your partner better?
- What methods did questioners use when they seemed stuck or nervous?
- What did you learn about subjects unfamiliar to you through this exercise?
- How did you use answers to help you ask additional questions?

- How did you feel about this exercise?
- What did you learn about yourself?
- What kinds of questions do your parents ask when you come home from school?
- What kinds of questions do you ask your parents?
- How do you feel when your friends don't ask questions about your feelings, activities, etc.?

8. Points to make about the learning activity:

- Individuals often are afraid to ask personal or open-ended questions because they think they are prying into another's life. However, many people are eager to have someone show that kind of interest in them.
- Asking effective questions is a critical skill in establishing a relationship with a shy or distrustful person.
- Frequently a person offers unsolicited information in answering a question. Many times, this unsolicited information is more important than the answer to your question. Use this "free" information as a bridge for developing the relationship.

CLOSING

9. Ask for the Observer's report. Allow time for individuals to react to the observations.

10. Ask, seek, knock. Give each student a 3×5 card with Matthew 7:7-8 copied on it: "Ask and it will be given to you; seek and you will find; knock and the door will be opened to you. For everyone who asks receives; he who seeks finds; and to him who knocks, the door will be opened."

Have the students read the cards. Say: "You've learned how to ask your peers questions in order to know them better and to draw them out. Asking caring questions isn't prying into someone's life. In peer ministry, asking caring questions helps hurting people see God's love in you. And, when you listen and question with care, you hear God in hurting people.

"God also wants you to ask *him* questions—to ask, seek and knock at the door." Ask students to turn over the 3×5 card and write an open-ended question to God. For example: "Lord, what do you have planned for my life?" "Lord, why do you feel so close at times and so far away at others?"

Ask students to stand and mingle, asking each other, "What are you seeking from God?" Emphasize the importance of listening to another. After hearing the response the listener should say, "God has heard your prayer."

When all have finished, gather in a circle and pray: "Lord, we thank you for hearing our questions. We ask that you give us wisdom and courage to ask caring questions in our ministry to our peers. In Jesus' name, amen."

*H*OMEWORK ASSIGNMENT . . .

Have students practice asking their family members open-ended or feeling-level questions. Or they could practice asking open-ended questions with a stranger they might meet in a store, bus, lunchroom, etc.

Conversational Skills: Listening

SESSION OBJECTIVES

Students will:

1. Recognize the difference between hearing and listening.

2. Identify the main points of a person's message based on content, feelings and tone of voice.

3. Participate in a simulated experience of information distortion.

4. Practice listening to and communicating with a partner.

SCRIPTURE FOUNDATION

Jesus Listens to the Samaritan Woman at the Well

Now he had to go through Samaria. So he came to a town in Samaria called Sychar, near the plot of ground Jacob had given to his son Joseph. Jacob's well was there, and Jesus, tired as he was from the journey, sat down by the well. It was about the sixth hour.

When a Samaritan woman came to draw water, Jesus said to her, "Will you give me a drink?" (His disciples had gone into the town to buy food.)

The Samaritan woman said to him, "You are a Jew and I am a Samaritan woman. How can you ask me for a drink?" (For Jews do not associate with Samaritans.)

Jesus answered her, "If you knew the gift of God and who it is that asks you for a drink, you would have asked him and he would have given you living water."

"Sir," the woman said, "you have nothing to draw with and the well is deep. Where can you get this living water? Are you greater than our father Jacob, who gave us the well and drank from it himself, as did also his sons and his flocks and herds?"

Jesus answered, "Everyone who drinks this water will be thirsty again, but whoever drinks the water I give him will never thirst. Indeed, the water I give him will become in him a spring of water welling up to eternal life."

The woman said to him, "Sir, give me this water so that I won't get thirsty and have to keep coming here to draw water."

He told her, "Go, call your husband and come back."

"I have no husband," she replied.

Jesus said to her, "You are right when you say you have no husband. The fact is, you have had five husbands, and the man you now have is not your husband. What you have just said is quite true."

"Sir," the woman said, "I can see that you are a prophet. Our fathers worshiped on this mountain, but you Jews claim that the place where we must worship is in Jerusalem."

Jesus declared, "Believe me, woman, a time is coming when you will worship the Father neither on this mountain nor in Jerusalem. You Samaritans worship what you do not know; we worship what we do know, for salvation is from the Jews. Yet a time is coming and has now come when the true worshipers will worship the Father in spirit and truth, for they are the kind of worshipers the Father seeks. God is spirit, and his worshipers must worship in spirit and in truth."

The woman said, "I know that Messiah" (called

*Christ) "is coming. When he comes, he will explain
everything to us."*
   Then Jesus declared, "I who speak to you am he."
                                          —John 4:4-26

The Samaritan woman at the well illustrates God's
gift of listening. After Jesus had asked the woman for
a drink of water, an intense conversation evolved between them on the pursuit for satisfaction in life, the
quality of relationships and beliefs about God. Eventually the conversation resulted in the woman's
conversion and in her witness to others.

The woman responded literally to the obvious
meaning of Jesus' questions and words. Jesus
responded to her with deeper meanings and implications of the questions and the words. Because he
brought this new dimension to the conversation,
Jesus made a permanent change in the woman's life.

Examine the dialogue in light of each person listening to the feelings and the underlying meanings of
words. It is critical in peer ministry that we look beyond the initially expressed verbal concerns. Effective
listening looks below the surface communication,
searching for the feelings and concerns of others.

We often look for someone to whom we can tell
our troubles, someone who will understand us, someone who will shield us against the cold winds of the
world, someone who will help us, comfort us, care
for us.

We want to be loved. But we are far less willing to
give the kind of love we want from others.

PREPARATION

1. Prepare the meeting area for the training group:
warm, comfortable and not too large or too small.
Obtain a chalkboard or newsprint pad, a tape recorder

and a blank tape.

2. Read carefully through the session, becoming fully prepared and aware of its objectives and learning activities.

3. To help you think through the purpose and direction of this session, answer the following questions either in writing or in thought:

● What kinds of people in my life do I find hard to listen to? Why?

● How often do I listen to the feelings of those in my family when they talk to me?

● Would I be considered a good listener by my husband or wife or children?

● Where do I need to improve?

● In what other ways did Jesus show how he could listen to people?

● How did his ability to listen change lives?

● Who is a good listener to me?

● What additional questions, points or examples can I use in making this lesson meaningful?

● Additional notes to myself:

Peer Ministry Training

OPENING

1. Pray. Open with a prayer by asking for God's guidance as participants seek to serve him.

2. Assign an Observer; and ask for homework reports.

3. Introduce the session. Ask:

● How many believe you are a good listener? Why?

 ● What is good listening?

 ● What can interfere with good listening?

Elton Mayo said, "One friend, one person who is truly understanding, who takes the trouble to listen to us as we consider our problems, can change our whole outlook on the world." All of us have experienced this in the rare times we have been in the company of an effective, genuine listener.

To care for others and understand them and their world, we must learn how to listen. Listening is not merely hearing words and feeding them back verbatim. Rather, listening is unlocking the door to other people's worlds, attempting to experience what they feel, and being conscious of the emphasis they put on certain words or ideas. Listening is helping others interpret what they're trying to communicate, then sharing what was heard to check for misunderstandings or incomplete ideas. This takes practice. Even more, it takes a desire to listen and a desire to elevate the interests of others above oneself. Listening involves putting aside for the moment one's own concerns and anxieties to concentrate on those of others.

4. Experience distorted or incomplete listening. Pick five people to participate in this demonstration. Ask one of them to stay in the room and ask the others to go outside, to be called in one by one.

Tell a "true life" story of a student with a problem. Give sufficient details so that the story is hard to remember. You can elaborate on this example: "Sarah is a junior in high school. She has two younger brothers. Her parents have been married for 20 years. Everyone thinks they are a happy, healthy family.

Sarah thought so too, until she learned her parents wanted a divorce. Sarah feels responsible for her parents' unhappiness. She blames herself for not detecting any warning signs throughout the years."

Say that you will record the description on tape as you read it. The student is to listen. When you are finished you will ask another student to come in and the first listener is to share with this new listener what was heard. This will also be recorded. When this has been done, the second listener shares with the third listener, and this is repeated until all five listeners have participated.

Before playing all the recordings back for the five listeners, ask for reactions from the five students:

● What made this difficult?
● How were you trying to listen?
● Were there any distractions?

Ask for group reactions:

● What did you hear that was consistently missed?
● What information began to be distorted?
● What information was consistently reported accurately?
● Did expression of feelings on the part of the information giver contribute to distortion? Explain.

Review these points about effective listening:

● You don't have to memorize what another says.
● You must be able to pick out relevant points.
● You cannot hear accurately if you are anxious or preoccupied.

SKILLS DEVELOPMENT

5. Share about important people. Divide students into pairs. One partner starts by describing an important person in his or her life. The important person may be admired by the speaker, have been an influence in some significant way, or have made life difficult. The person may be a relative, coach, teacher, pastor, friend, etc. The listener can ask questions for clarification, asking particularly for the meaning of vague words or phrases the speaker may have used.

Students may say no one is important in their life. Help them get started by saying that "important" means different things to different people. If they can't think of anyone, then have them talk about someone in their lives such as a parent or teacher.

If you observe that a listener is showing no interest, being rude or making it difficult for the speaker, intervene. Talk about what you observed. Relate this observation to peer ministry and caring for others even when we don't know them. What message is the listener giving by his or her behavior? If this does not help, ask the pair to stop and observe others. Bring up the subject during the Response time.

When the speaker finishes, the listener should tell the speaker what was heard in his or her own words. The objective is not to repeat a detailed account. Rather, the skill is repeating the *heart of the message* given, particularly the feeling level of what was shared.

After 10 minutes have the partners reverse roles.

RESPONSE

Use the following questions for debriefing this activity and helping students respond to what they have experienced. Questions under the "Necessary transition questions" section should always be asked. The points you want to emphasize are summarized following the questions.

6. Necessary transition questions:

● What went through your mind when you were told to talk about an important person in your life? Were you pleased? nervous? confused? Why?

● What made it difficult for you as a listener?

7. Examining the experience:

● In what specific ways did your listener show he or she was listening to you?

● What behaviors or questions of the listener made it more difficult to talk about your person?

● Did your listener's questions or sharing what he or she heard help you understand more clearly why your person is important to you?

● What suggestions could you give to your listener to help him or her be a better listener?

● What feelings were "heard" in what a partner shared?

● In what ways did you acknowledge those feelings?

● How would you rate yourself as a listener at this point?

8. Points to make about the learning activity:

● Since this is a learning situation, encourage students to give constructive criticism to other group members. Students may be reluctant to say anything that may seem critical. Or they may be destructively critical. Both behaviors need attention.

● Frequently people feel they have been listened to if some response is given to the feelings behind the words.

● Often a speaker is unsure of how to express an idea or describe a characteristic. This happens especially when a person talks about a problem. The listener can help the speaker by asking clarifying questions or restating an idea in different words.

CLOSING

9. Ask for the Observer's report. Allow time for individuals to react to the observations.

10. Be still, and know that I am God. Explore the value of listening to God. Say: "All of your life you will have problems; at times the problems will distract you from what is most important in life: listening to God. In your ministry to peers, you will need energy to really listen to others. Your preoccupations, problems and hassles will affect your ability to listen. Every day you need to refocus your priorities—by listening to God."

Point out to the students that peer ministers are not to be God's "busybodies for the kingdom." Rather, peer ministers are to have the "listening factor." Read the story of Mary and Martha from Luke 10:38-42. Say: "In peer ministry you will be tempted to do everything for everybody. But none of us can—in fact, we lose effectiveness for God as we stretch ourselves thinner. Peer ministry is listening—to hurting people, yes—but first listening to God."

Stand in a circle and put arms on shoulders. Ask students to close their eyes and concentrate on listening to God. Lead a guided prayer with the following model, allowing for plenty of silence between petitions:

"Lord, like Martha, we are worried and upset about many things. We lift those worries to you now . . .

"Lord, in Psalms you say, 'Be still, and know that I am God.' We take a moment of silence and feel your presence . . .

"Lord, you've called us to care for others with our ears—to listen to your people. Help us to listen now as we voice our concerns to you and each other . . ." (You go first.)

"Lord, help us silence the noise of everyday problems and hassles and listen to you . . .

"Lord, thanks for listening. In the name of your Son, amen."

HOMEWORK ASSIGNMENT . . .

Ask students to listen to their teachers throughout the week or to a discussion on television, particularly paying attention to the feelings behind the words and the kinds of words the speaker uses most frequently. Students should summarize in their minds what the speaker was saying.

Another option is to have each student listen to a member of the family or a friend and practice giving feedback to what was heard. The student should notice what happens in the conversation as this is done.

Non-Verbal Communication

SESSION OBJECTIVES

Students will:

1. Interpret the meaning of non-verbal communication.

2. Listen to words and observe non-verbal behavior, then interpret the combined message to the speaker.

3. Share personal concerns and listen to others' concerns.

4. Observe a demonstration of the speaker, listener and observer roles.

5. Work in triads, practicing each of these roles with a personal concern.

SCRIPTURE FOUNDATION

The Lord Turned and Looked Straight at Peter

Then seizing him, they led him away and took him into the house of the high priest. Peter followed at a distance. But when they had kindled a fire in the middle of the courtyard and had sat down together, Peter sat down with them. A servant girl saw him seated there in the firelight. She looked closely at him and said, "This man was with him."

*But he denied it. "Woman, I don't know him," he
said.*

*A little later someone else saw him and said, "You
also are one of them."*

"Man, I am not!" Peter replied.

*About an hour later another asserted, "Certainly
this fellow was with him, for he is a Galilean."*

*Peter replied, "Man, I don't know what you're
talking about!" Just as he was speaking, the rooster
crowed. The Lord turned and looked straight at
Peter. Then Peter remembered the word the Lord had
spoken to him: "Before the rooster crows today, you
will disown me three times." And he went outside
and wept bitterly.*

—Luke 22:54-62

This lesson focuses on observing non-verbal indicators of feelings and emotions. The lesson deals with recognizing feelings and looking beyond words to a more accurate interpretation of the message.

In the previous session, the story of the Samaritan woman at the well illustrated how Jesus listened to the feelings of her message. We do not know her facial expressions or her tone of voice, but it is obvious that Jesus knew how to gauge her non-verbal communication. This story is a good reference for this session.

The Luke 22 passage shows Jesus' ability to look beyond behavior to the real person. Peter had denied Jesus three times—because of the pressure of the situation. After Peter had denied him three times (as predicted), the Lord turned his head and looked straight at Peter. At this point Peter realized what he had done and knew that the Lord fully understood him, including his weaknesses.

Listening to verbal and non-verbal communication involves hearing the feelings, motivations and messages that are not expressed by words alone.

John 2:12-17, the cleansing of the temple, shows the suitability of expressing one's feelings. Jesus effectively communicated his emotions through a non-verbal expression. Many troubled people feel they should not express emotions. By using this passage one can introduce the advantage and desirability of expressing emotions.

There are many other passages that deal with symbolic and non-verbal expressions of care and the meaning of relationships. For example, read the stories of the woman using rare perfume to anoint Jesus' feet (John 12:1-11) and Judas' kiss in the Garden of Gethsemane (Matthew 26:47-50). These examples and others have obvious meanings and not-so-obvious underlying meanings. This session looks at the latter.

*P*REPARATION

1. Prepare the meeting area for the training group: warm, comfortable and not too large or too small. Obtain a chalkboard or newsprint pad. Photocopy a "Please Hear What I'm Not Saying" handout for each person.

2. Read carefully through the session, becoming fully prepared and aware of its objectives and learning activities.

3. To help you think through the purpose and direction of this session, answer the following questions either in writing or in thought:

● How often am I willing to talk about my problems or concerns with others?

● What keeps me from doing this?

● Whom do I seek for consultation and help on a problem?

● What is it about these people that makes them effective?

● What concern will I share with this group?

● What non-verbal messages does my church send during worship? What is the meaning of each?

● What non-verbal expressions of care do people show us?

● What non-verbal acts of hatred or anger do people use?

● Which is more prevalent: care or hatred?

● What additional questions, points or examples can I use in making this lesson meaningful?

● Additional notes to myself:

Peer Ministry Training

OPENING

1. Pray. Open with a prayer by asking for God's guidance as participants seek to serve him.

2. Assign an Observer; and ask for homework reports.

3. Introduce the concept of non-verbal communication. Ask:

● When you get home from school, or when your parents get home, how can you tell what kind of day your father or mother has had, even before he or she says anything? What specific behaviors do they show?

● How can you tell how your teachers, coaches or youth workers are feeling as they walk into the room, before they say anything?

● What clues do you use to interpret the mood or

feelings of other students you see walking around school, including students you don't know?

● How do repeated examples of behavior help you understand what these behaviors mean?

● How does familiarity with another help you understand his or her communication habits?

Our accuracy in understanding and interpreting non-verbal messages increases when we have repeated samples of a person's behaviors. Without practice in recognizing non-verbal messages, we may miss or misinterpret the meaning of them.

SKILLS DEVELOPMENT

4. Triads. Divide the group into small groups of exactly three people. Each small group will have a speaker, listener and observer. (If your group isn't divisible by three, assign two observers for some of the small groups.) Members will take turns participating in each role. Announce that you will demonstrate today's activity after you give the following instructions.

Explain that everyone will do three different things:

● *Share* something about themselves that they would like to change;

● *Listen* to another talk about a behavior he or she would like to change; and

● *Observe* each person sharing and listening.

For this activity to be a true learning experience, each student must select a behavior he or she really wants to change. Perhaps he or she has even struggled with it.

The listener is to ask questions to clarify the meaning if it isn't clear, and feed back what he or she heard. Again, the listener shouldn't repeat the exact words, but interpret the meaning of those words. The listener is *not* to counsel the speaker.

When the speaker is satisfied that the listener understands, then the observer, who has observed both speaker and listener, will share what non-verbal behaviors were used by both. The observer does not participate in the listening feedback.

When all three have finished, shift roles and repeat the activity. Shift again, and do the final round so that each person has practiced each role.

After you give these instructions, ask students to brainstorm various behaviors that concern people. Assist group members by giving some examples.

Before students begin the activity, demonstrate it. If there is an adult co-leader, he or she should participate. For the third member, pick a student to assist as listener. If you are the only adult, ask two students to help. Explain that this is difficult to do, especially in front of a group. Take the role of speaker.

Demonstrate only the first round of the activity. When finished, ask the listener how he or she felt. What was difficult for the observer?

Make sure the groups understand the activity.

For this activity to be successful, it is imperative that you share a *real* heart-felt concern. Even though as an adult you may not feel young people will understand the full meaning of the concern, they will understand your feelings about it. This will help their willingness to risk sharing a personal concern.

Share any reactions you had in doing this in front of a group. Perhaps admit how hard it is to talk about yourself when you aren't proud of a behavior.

Have the triads begin the activity. Walk around the room to make sure everyone understands and has started. About every 10 minutes ask groups to shift roles.

Wait until all groups have finished before calling everyone back into a large group. Some may want to continue because they are involved in something meaningful. If this happens, let them continue.

RESPONSE

Use the following questions for debriefing this activity and helping students respond to what they have experienced. Questions under the "Necessary transition questions" section should always be asked. The points you want to emphasize are summarized following the questions.

5. Necessary transition questions:
● Which role was the hardest for you? Why?
● Which was the easiest? Why?
● What did you learn about your strengths and weaknesses as a speaker, a listener and an observer?

6. Examining the experience:
Speaker:
● What was hardest about sharing a concern with another? How did it feel?
● What did the listener say or do that helped you better understand your concern?
Listener:
● What made it difficult for you to accurately understand the concern?
● Is it helpful to listen to another when you immediately relate his or her concern to your personal experience or a similar concern? When could this interfere with listening?
● What direct or indirect advice did you give?
Observer:
● What helped the understanding between the speaker and listener?
● What decreased the understanding between them?
● What repeated behaviors did each person use in practicing his or her roles?
● What behaviors revealed most clearly the feel-

ings of the speaker or the listener?

● What did you learn about your own behavior when *you* were observed?

7. Points to make about the learning activity:

● It is almost always hard, and sometimes painful, to talk about a problem or personal concern. By participating in the learning activity, peer ministers will grow more sensitive to what hurting people go through.

● There is a difference between a "head" concern (one that a person thinks he or she should be concerned about, but may actually not be) and a "heart" concern (when emotions are involved). The "heart" concern reveals itself more often through non-verbal behaviors.

● A listener may assume he or she is familiar with a concern because of experiencing a similar one. Consequently, the listener may stop picking up important clues to the intended message.

● A speaker can understand the concern more clearly by hearing how it sounded to the listener, correcting a misunderstanding and stating the concern in a different way.

● Sometimes a listener tends to interrupt and share a similar problem, taking the focus off the speaker. How does this interfere in counseling another?

● Observers sometimes reluctantly share observations because they feel it is criticizing, rather than helping, another.

● Sometimes observers get so involved in listening to the words that they miss important non-verbal observations.

CLOSING

8. Ask for the Observer's report. Allow time for individuals to react to the observations.

9. "Please Hear What I'm Not Saying." Ask six students to help you present the "Please Hear What I'm Not Saying" handout. Pass out copies to all students. Give them a minute to read through the poem. Then read the poem in order, the first student reading the first section, and so on. You will read the last section, which begins, "Who am I? you may wonder."

After the reading of the poem, say: "Awareness of non-verbal communication equips you with new 'ears' to hear and new 'eyes' to see hurting people around you. Peer ministry calls you to risk your pride and your tendency not to get involved. The rewards are worth the risks—in the process of helping others, *you* are also helped and changed to more of a Christ-likeness."

For a closing prayer, ask students to affirm one another in a caring, non-verbal way by looking each person in the eyes and then giving a hug. Make sure each person gets hugged. When all have been hugged, say "amen."

HOMEWORK ASSIGNMENT . . .

Ask students to observe each person in one of their classes throughout the week. Students should take notes of behaviors that indicate shyness, anger, depression, nervousness, self-confidence, etc. Have members do the same for friends during the lunch period. Explain that observing friends in group social situations could reveal behaviors different from one-to-one situations.

HANDOUT:

Please Hear What I'm Not Saying

Student 1:

Don't be fooled by me.
Don't be fooled by the face I wear.
For I wear a mask, I wear a thousand masks.
Masks that I am afraid to take off.
But none of them is me.
Pretending is an art that's second nature to me.
But don't be fooled.
I give you the impression that I am secure,
That all is sunny and unruffled with me,
Within as well as without,
That confidence is my name and coolness is my game,
And that I need no one.
Don't believe me! Please!

Student 2:

My surface may be smooth,
But my surface is my mask,
My varying and ever concealing mask.
Beneath lies no smugness,
No complacence.
Beneath dwells the real me,
In confusion and fear,
In loneliness.

Student 3:

I idly chatter with you in the cool tones of surface talk.
I tell you everything that's really nothing.
But I don't tell you what's crying within me.
So, when I'm going through my routine,
Please don't be fooled by what I'm saying.
Please listen carefully, and try to hear what I'm *not* saying,
And what I'd like to be able to say,
What for *survival* I need to say,
But what I can't say.

(continued on next page)

Student 4:
Only you can call me into aliveness,
Each time you're kind, and gentle, and encouraging,
Each time you try to understand.
Because you really care,
My heart begins to grow wings.
Very small wings, very feeble wings.
Wings to help me soar.

Student 5:
With your sympathy and sensitivity, and
Your power of understanding,
You can breathe life into me.
I want you to know that.
I want you to know how important you are to me.
How you can wake up the person that is me—if you choose to.
Please choose to!
Do not pass me by!

Student 6:
It will not be easy for you.
My long conviction of worthlessness builds strong walls.
The nearer you come to me, the blinder I may strike back.
I fight against the very thing I cry out for.
But I am told that love is stronger than strong walls.
In this lies my hope.
My only hope.

Leader:
Who am I? you may wonder.
I am someone you know very well.
I am a hurting member of your family,
I am the person sitting beside you in this room,
I am every person you meet on the street.
Please don't believe my mask,
Please come behind it to glimpse the real me.
Please speak to me, share a little of yourself with me.
At least *recognize* me!

Because you care.

—Author unknown

Welcoming a Stranger to a Group

SESSION OBJECTIVES

Students will:

1. Learn to make a stranger comfortable and welcome in a group.

2. Learn how to adapt their behavior to deal with unexpected events.

3. Simulate welcoming a stranger into the group.

SCRIPTURE FOUNDATION

When Did We See You a Stranger?

"When the Son of Man comes in his glory, and all the angels with him, he will sit on his throne in heavenly glory. All the nations will be gathered before him, and he will separate the people one from another as a shepherd separates the sheep from the goats. He will put the sheep on his right and the goats on his left.

"Then the King will say to those on his right, 'Come, you who are blessed by my Father; take your inheritance, the kingdom prepared for you since the creation of the world. For I was hungry and you gave me something to eat, I was thirsty and you gave me something to drink, I was a stranger and you invited me in, I needed clothes and you clothed me, I was sick and you looked after me, I was in prison

and you came to visit me.'

"Then the righteous will answer him, 'Lord, when did we see you hungry and feed you, or thirsty and give you something to drink? When did we see you a stranger and invite you in, or needing clothes and clothe you? When did we see you sick or in prison and go to visit you?'

"The King will reply, 'I tell you the truth, whatever you did for one of the least of these brothers of mine, you did for me.' "

—Matthew 25:31-40

The Bible contains many references to welcoming strangers and helping others in need. When the love of Christ is alive within our hearts, we will respond to people with a different perception. No longer will others seem "invisible." Like the righteous in this passage, no one will be a stranger to us.

Jesus made it clear that a Christian's first priority is to reach out to others, especially one to one. "This is my command: Love each other" (John 15:17). The responsibility for welcoming a stranger is ours, not the stranger's. For example, Zacchaeus showed interest—but it was Jesus who welcomed him (Luke 19:1-10). We do to another what we would want done to ourselves if we were the stranger.

What would we like done to us if we were strangers entering a group? We would want someone to welcome us—someone willing to risk rejection by the group. This person would offer his or her time to us and introduce us to the group.

Welcoming a stranger is risky. Jesus invited Zacchaeus to dinner—a man considered unacceptable by the prestigious or "in" group. Jesus' fellowship opened the door of faith to Zacchaeus. When we risk showing love and fellowship we demonstrate our commitment to the Lord.

PREPARATION

1. Prepare the meeting area for the training group: warm, comfortable and not too large or too small. Obtain a chalkboard or newsprint pad.

2. Read carefully through the session, becoming fully prepared and aware of its objectives and learning activities.

3. To help you think through the purpose and direction of this session, answer the following questions either in writing or in thought:

- How have I behaved in a group when a stranger came in?
- Have I ever deliberately made a stranger feel unwelcome?
- What keeps me from making a stranger feel welcome?
- What ways did Jesus use to make a person feel welcome?
- Who did Jesus reach out to most often?
- What might be difficult for my group during this session?
- What is the most important thing for students to learn from this session?
- What additional questions, points or examples can I use in making this lesson meaningful?
- Additional notes to myself:

Peer Ministry Training

OPENING

1. Pray. Open with a prayer by asking for God's guidance as participants seek to serve him.

2. Assign an Observer; and ask for homework reports.

3. Read Matthew 25:31-40. Point out Jesus' reference to welcoming a stranger. For a creative paraphrase of this passage, use the "Jesus at Your High School" cut from *"Get Off My Roof!" and Other Faith-Building Stories* by Thom Schultz (Group).

4. Lock-out. This learning activity helps young people experience firsthand how it feels to try to get in a group or to keep someone out. Pick one person to stand to the side while the group stands in a circle and locks arms. The group members should do everything they can (without physically hurting anyone) to keep the outsider from getting into the circle. The outsider should do everything he or she can to get inside.

Allow the activity to go on for no more than 30 seconds. By this time, the outsider has overpowered the group, or most often, the outsider cannot get in and usually gives up. Pick two or three others to be the outsider and give it a try. Then ask the following questions:

Outsiders:

● If you didn't get into the group, how did it feel? Why did you give up? Did you feel anger or bitterness? Explain.

● If you did get in, what method did you use to force your way in? How did you feel once you got in? Was it worth the effort? Did you feel genuinely accepted? Explain.

Insiders:

● How did you feel as you kept the person out? superior? content? playful?

● Were you more aware of the outsider's feelings or the need to band together?

SKILLS DEVELOPMENT

5. Introduce the skill of welcoming a stranger. Ask:

● How many of you have ever been a stranger in some group? moved into a new town? joined a new club or organization?

● What happened when you were new? What did people do?

● How did you feel? How did the lock-out relate to your experience?

● What was particularly good about your experience as a stranger? What was particularly bad?

● As you think about your experience, how could you help a new person feel comfortable in a group?

6. Simulated experience welcoming a stranger. Explain that sometimes in a group we behave differently from when we are alone or with another person. We find ourselves saying or doing things because of group pressure.

Say, "To help you understand these situations and to increase your understanding of how to help a stranger or someone in a group, we will practice welcoming a stranger." Divide into groups of about five. Have each group select someone to be the stranger. No one may volunteer; the group must choose the stranger.

The stranger is to leave the room. While he or she is gone, the members should decide the setting for the group. Is it a club? a neighborhood? a classroom? What role is the stranger to play in this simulation?

Once the group members decide the setting, they should plan what they will do as a group to *welcome* the stranger. When they have a strategy, someone from the group is to bring the stranger in, telling him or her the role to play. Then the group should enact the simulation.

If a group is slow in selecting a stranger, or in planning a strategy, give this group your assistance. After 10 or 15 minutes, bring the groups together.

*R*ESPONSE

Use the following questions for debriefing this activity and helping students respond to what they have experienced. Questions under the "Necessary transition questions" section should always be asked. The points you want to emphasize are summarized following the questions.

7. Necessary transition questions:

Strangers:

● How were you chosen? How did you feel about the method used?

● How did you feel when you were standing outside, waiting to be called in?

● If you felt fear, why?

● What was the setting for the group? What role were you to play?

● What specific things did the group do to make you feel welcome?

● What specific things did the group do to make you feel nervous, uncomfortable or unwelcome?

● What did you learn from this activity?

Group members:

● What plans had you made for welcoming your stranger?

● Did you carry them out? If not, why?

● What did you do unknowingly that made the

stranger feel uncomfortable? A frequent experience is an interrogation, in which each person takes a turn asking the stranger a question.

● Was there a chair for the stranger? Did the group share anything about itself? Did one or two people do all the talking?

● What did you learn from this activity?

8. Examining the experience:

● Where have you learned unkind behaviors toward strangers?

● Describe the power of negative pressure in a group setting.

● What could one individual within a group do to turn an unfriendly group into a warm, accepting one?

● Do past unsuccessful experiences build defensiveness within a stranger? Why?

9. Points to make about the learning activity:

● Sometimes people feel they always come up losers—they expect rejection and see themselves as strangers.

● Some people lack the skills to get into a group. What others might see as anti-social behaviors are really desperate attempts to belong.

● Jesus made it clear that Christians are to welcome new people into the group. If we know this, why do youth groups often fall short in welcoming new kids? Because we are human—but we have a great God who empowers us.

● Group members risk a lot of comfortable "in" group coziness by welcoming strangers. But what would happen if a group *never* welcomed a stranger? The group would eventually die.

● Sometimes when people are rejected (forced to be strangers) by a group, they form their own group or become actively hostile to the original group. Peer ministers need to realize that they might represent the original group to someone who has been rejected.

CLOSING

10. Ask for the Observer's report. Allow time for individuals to react to the observations.

11. "A Reconciliation Experience." To experience reconciliation in a visual way, gather the group members in a circle for this closing devotion. Have them place their arms around each other. You are to start by talking about the enjoyment and pleasure of being a part of a group and sharing the closeness that a group offers. Then acknowledge that while the potential for being a real group and sharing closeness with each other always exists, sometimes we separate ourselves and can't enjoy the love God intends.

Continue by saying, "To show you what I mean, I would like everyone in the circle who has been a part of a group and has ever let that group down, to drop your arms from another's shoulders." After a brief period of silence, continue the activity as follows.

You say:	*Action:*
Sometimes we say things that are harmful to other people.	I would like anyone who has ever said something that was harmful to another member of a group to take a step backward.

Silence

Often we exclude others from our group.	If anyone has ever excluded another person from a group or made someone feel left out, please take another step backward.

Silence

Sometimes we say things that aren't true. We deny making a mistake, or we are afraid to tell somebody something.

If this has ever happened to you, I would like you to turn and face away from the center of the circle.

Silence

Sometimes we have pretended not to see the needs of other people.

If there have been times that you have ignored the needs of other people and remained apart from them, I would like you to close your eyes.

Silence

We were meant to be together, yet at times our actions kept us apart.

If you have ever helped someone with a need they had, I would like you to turn around.

Silence

It is important to listen to people.

If you have ever taken the time to listen to a friend who had a problem, I would like you to take one step toward the circle.

Silence

The best gift we can give people is to welcome them and make them feel included.

If you have ever made someone feel welcome and a part of things, open your eyes.

Silence

Confession to one another can tear down walls.	If you have ever shared a way that you have failed someone, even if it was hard to do, then take another step in toward the circle.

Silence

God asks us to forgive one another.	If you have ever forgiven someone, then place your arms around the people beside you.

A group hug would be an appropriate ending.

"A Reconciliation Experience" is from *The Giving Book: A Creative Resource for Senior High Ministry* by Paul M. Thompson & Joani Schultz, 1985. Copyright John Knox Press. Used by permission.

*H*OMEWORK ASSIGNMENT . . .

Ask students to persuade someone sitting alone in the lunchroom to join them and their friends for the lunch hour. Or, if they see someone alone at school, youth group or any other activity, invite him or her to join their group, even if the rest of the group doesn't like the idea.

Decision-Making and Values

SESSION OBJECTIVES

Students will:

1. Understand what it means to counsel.

2. Understand the importance of personal goals and values in changing behavior.

3. Clarify personal values.

SCRIPTURE FOUNDATION

The Rich Young Man

Now a man came up to Jesus and asked, "Teacher, what good thing must I do to get eternal life?"

"Why do you ask me about what is good?" Jesus replied. "There is only One who is good. If you want to enter life, obey the commandments."

"Which ones?" the man inquired.

Jesus replied, " 'Do not murder, do not commit adultery, do not steal, do not give false testimony, honor your father and mother,' and 'love your neighbor as yourself.' "

"All these I have kept," the young man said. "What do I still lack?"

Jesus answered, "If you want to be perfect, go, sell your possessions and give to the poor, and you will have treasure in heaven. Then come, follow me."

When the young man heard this, he went away

sad, because he had great wealth.

Then Jesus said to his disciples, "I tell you the truth, it is hard for a rich man to enter the kingdom of heaven. Again I tell you, it is easier for a camel to go through the eye of a needle than for a rich man to enter the kingdom of God."

When the disciples heard this, they were greatly astonished and asked, "Who then can be saved?"

Jesus looked at them and said, "With man this is impossible, but with God all things are possible."

Peter answered him, "We have left everything to follow you! What then will there be for us?"

Jesus said to them, "I tell you the truth, at the renewal of all things, when the Son of Man sits on his glorious throne, you who have followed me will also sit on twelve thrones, judging the twelve tribes of Israel. And everyone who has left houses or brothers or sisters or father or mother or children or fields for my sake will receive a hundred times as much and will inherit eternal life. But many who are first will be last, and many who are last will be first."

—Matthew 19:16-30

This passage points to various dimensions of values that distinguish the Christian from the non-believer. It deals with possessions, anxiety, concern for others, and how our inner lives determine the kind of people we really are. In secular values-clarification exercises, individuals are led to reach for what the world values. Perhaps a Christian's most significant task is to examine his or her actions for values that reflect Christ's model and teaching.

W.E. Sangster writes, "When things become the chief purpose of living, when money is seen as life's chief good, every precious thing is in danger—the integrity of the individual soul, the decency of the community, the soundness of all human life."

Reliance upon possessions is the temptation of the "haves." Debilitating anxiety is the snare set in the path of the "have-nots." The real cure of needless concern over possessions is to have a true scale of values. Fulton Sheen writes: "To conquer anxiety does not mean eliminating our desires, but, rather, arranging them in a hierarchy as our Lord reminded us when he said that life is more than the raiment. A religious man overcomes anxiety by making all material things subject to the human, by disciplining the body until it is subject to the spirit, and by submitting the whole personality to God."

Wealth is not the only factor that can separate a person from his or her neighbor and therefore from God. The use of spare time also has a potential to separate us from others and God. How much do we use our time in service to the lonely? We may be blessed with an abundance of comforts. How much personal ease are we willing to forego to help the less privileged?

Some of us are too busy to give and receive affection, too preoccupied to seek quietness, too ambitious to drop out of the race for success, in order to give priority to more lasting values. This session looks at putting first things first.

*P*REPARATION

1. Prepare the meeting area for the training group: warm, comfortable and not too large or too small. Obtain a chalkboard or newsprint pad. Photocopy a "Christian Value-Ranking" handout for each person.

2. Read carefully through the session, becoming fully prepared and aware of its objectives and learning activities.

3. To help you think through the purpose and direction of this session, answer the following questions either in writing or in thought:

● How do I feel about making my own decisions?

- What does my use of time say about my values?
- What do I value least? most?
- What additional questions, points or examples can I use in making this lesson meaningful?
- Additional notes to myself:

Peer Ministry Training

OPENING

1. Pray. Open with a prayer by asking for God's guidance as participants seek to serve him.

2. Since this is basically a discussion session, no Observer will be assigned. Ask for homework reports.

3. Introduce the learning activities. Ask:

- What do you think you will be doing as a peer minister?
- What is your definition of counseling?
- What is the difference between giving advice and counseling?
- Why might it be more difficult to counsel another, rather than just give him or her advice?

SKILLS DEVELOPMENT—PART 1

4. Decision Agent. Tell students they are about to participate in a type of fantasy. The more seriously they take this, the more they will learn from the exercise.

Explain: "We often go to 'experts' to ask for advice. We go to guidance counselors, radio repairmen, travel agents, parents and so on. Sometimes we tell this expert what we want to happen, how much we can spend, what we don't want to do, etc.

"There is a new expert around who is skilled in making personal decisions. He is called the Decision Agent. Although he is neither clairvoyant nor divine, sometimes he can predict the future. He knows more alternatives than we know, has information we don't have, and can estimate the best alternative for an individual as long as he knows what that person wants. He is always concerned for our welfare.

"Since he is very much in demand, he has time to make only three decisions for us."

Ask students to presume that they must turn over three personal decisions of their lives to this Decision Agent. These are decisions they currently are facing or will face in the future. Students are *not* just asking for information; they are turning over those three decisions to the Agent. They will do what the Agent decides.

Say that because this Agent couldn't possibly make a decision for the students' welfare without knowing some of their values, participants should write on their papers the following:

● The three decisions they want to give away to the Agent; and

● The information the Agent would need to know to make the decisions in their best interests.

After about five minutes, say that a new law has been passed. *All* personal decisions must be turned over to the Agent, with the exception of three. Which three decisions would students keep?

Allow a few minutes for the kids to decide. Be prepared for angry or strong emotion in this exercise. Appreciate it. The more the emotion, the more students are experiencing the importance of making their own decisions. When the group has finished, write "Given Away" and "Keep" on the board or newsprint.

RESPONSE

Use the following questions for debriefing this activity and helping students respond to what they have experienced. Questions under the "Necessary transition questions" section should always be asked. The points you want to emphasize are summarized following the questions.

5. Necessary transition questions:

● Which category was the hardest to fill out and why?

● What decisions did you give away?

● What decisions did you keep?

6. Examining the experience:

● Reflect on any differences between the two categories of decisions based on the examples given. Why might this be so?

● We have limited hours in each day. Making a good decision requires time to collect important information. Which decisions seem most important?

● What is the difference between those decisions listed as "Given Aways" and those as "Keeps"?

7. Points to make about the learning activity:

● We are often decision agents for others and we usually think we are doing it for their welfare.

● Many people do not want to give away *any* of their decisions. But often they don't know how to make decisions.

● It is important to reflect on a person's anger when he or she has to give up some personal decisions.

● Usually the "Given Away" decisions have fewer

long-range consequences than the "Keeps," which involve deeper values that would be hard to express to a Decision Agent.

● People don't want to give away their decisions. This is critical in counseling. Most people go to a counselor for a decision. An effective counselor does not give advice; rather, he or she helps the person look at consequences and explore possible alternatives, with the counselee making the final decision.

● People reserve the right to fail. Peer ministers succeed when they reach out, not by making sure a peer makes "the right" decision.

● Read this quote from *Alice in Wonderland* by Lewis Carroll:

> *When Alice was wandering in Wonderland, she came to a crossroads where she met the Cheshire Cat. "Which path should I take from here?" asked Alice.*
> *The cat replied, "That depends on where you want to get to."*
> *"I don't much care where," said Alice.*
> *"Then it doesn't matter which path you take," said the Cat.*

● As counselors, we must help counselees determine where they want to get to. Our task is not to tell them which path they should take.

SKILLS DEVELOPMENT—PART 2

8. "Christian Value-Ranking." Since values play such an important part in deciding where one wants to get to, it is important for a peer minister to understand his or her own values.

Distribute a "Christian Value-Ranking" handout to each person.

When the group has finished, ask each person to share, if he or she is willing, the top-ranked value and why he or she values it. Do the same for the lowest value.

RESPONSE

Use the following questions for debriefing this activity and helping students respond to what they have experienced. Questions under the "Necessary transition questions" section should always be asked. The points you want to emphasize are summarized following the questions.

9. Necessary transition questions:

● If you could eliminate the two lowest-ranked items on your sheet, how would you feel?

● To what extent have you achieved your top-ranked item?

● Would your best friend know you value this item so much? Explain.

10. Examining the experience:

● How does your behavior coincide with your ranking?

● How does this exercise apply to effectiveness in peer ministry?

11. Points to make about the learning activity:

● Some students may have chosen the same item for different reasons. These reasons are the most important indicators of values.

● People often say they value something because they think it will be socially acceptable, not because they truly value it. This is frequently a problem in getting to the core of a counselee's problem.

● Regardless of whether a peer minister agrees with a value, that person needs to help a counselee clarify exactly what he or she wants in resolving a problem.

● When this has been done, often the counselee knows which path to take.

● Perhaps the most important task of a peer minister is to help a counselee clarify desired outcomes.

Closing

12. If anyone chooses to do God's will . . .
Help peer ministers value the role they fulfill in God's plan. Say: "You signed up for peer ministry training because you wanted to. No one forced you; you decided to. I believe that says great things about your values and Christian commitment. God does not force us to respond to his grace—that's up to us."

Read John 7:16-18:

> *Jesus answered, "My teaching is not my own. It comes from him who sent me. If anyone chooses to do God's will, he will find out whether my teaching comes from God or whether I speak on my own. He who speaks on his own does so to gain honor for himself, but he who works for the honor of the one who sent him is a man of truth; there is nothing false about him."*

To help students affirm each other and understand how choices affect friendship, ask them to voice responses to the statement "A friend chooses to . . ." Ask that the values be phrased with a personal response such as "be there when I need him," "listen to me," or "love me when I am unlovable." List these values on the board or newsprint. Be sure to list verbatim these values as they're expressed and offer no comments.

After everyone has had a chance to contribute to the list, say: "Let's look at the characteristics of Jesus. As we look at the values we most appreciate in our friends, let's exchange 'a friend' for 'Jesus' in front of each one."

Go through the entire list, asking the students to read aloud the values. The previous examples would change to: "Jesus chooses to be there when I need him," "Jesus chooses to listen to me," and "Jesus chooses to love me when I am unlovable."

Say that the characteristics of good friends are the same ones we find in Christ. When we are good friends to others, we represent Christ to them.

Stand in a circle with arms around shoulders. Ask each student to affirm the person on his or her right by completing the sentence "(Name) represents Christ to me because . . ." You go first. After going around the circle, say "amen."

(Editor's note: The closing activity above was adapted from the "Jesus Is . . ." activity in *Spiritual Growth in Youth Ministry*, copyright © 1985 by J. David Stone, published by Group Books.)

*H*OMEWORK ASSIGNMENT . . .

Ask students to record the major ways in which they spend their time and money in the coming week. Ask them to identify their top three values indicated by their use of time and money.

HANDOUT:

Christian Value-Ranking

Rank the following items from first to last in their importance to you. What is the most important to you? second most? and so on. Try to rank what is important to *you*, not what others say is important.

_____ One or several good friends.

_____ Money to go to movies, buy lunches and so on.

_____ A high grade-point average.

_____ A boyfriend or girlfriend.

_____ Lots of free time to do whatever I want.

_____ A good relationship with my parents.

_____ A large home with a lot of comforts.

_____ Time to grow in my Christian faith.

_____ Be a good athlete.

_____ Learn many new things.

_____ Help my friends and family.

_____ Honesty with family, friends and schoolwork.

_____ Be trusted by my parents.

_____ A good-looking body.

Sharing Your Christian Faith

SESSION OBJECTIVES

Students will:

1. Learn to express clearly what they believe.

2. Learn to identify and overcome their fears about sharing their faith.

3. Learn to talk about personal faith without using technical theological terms.

4. Share what is most meaningful about their faith.

5. Practice talking to a difficult or critical person about their faith.

SCRIPTURE FOUNDATION

We Are Not Ashamed of the Gospel

Then he said to them all: "If anyone would come after me, he must deny himself and take up his cross daily and follow me. For whoever wants to save his life will lose it, but whoever loses his life for me will save it. What good is it for a man to gain the whole world, and yet lose or forfeit his very self? If anyone is ashamed of me and my words, the Son of Man will be ashamed of him when he comes in his glory and in the glory of the Father and of the holy angels."

—Luke 9:23-26

We Love Because He First Loved Us

God is love. Whoever lives in love lives in God, and God in him. In this way love is made complete among us so that we will have confidence on the day of judgment, because in this world we are like him. There is no fear in love. But perfect love drives out fear, because fear has to do with punishment. The one who fears is not made perfect in love.

We love because he first loved us. If anyone says, "I love God," yet hates his brother, he is a liar. For anyone who does not love his brother, whom he has seen, cannot love God, whom he has not seen. And he has given us this command: Whoever loves God must also love his brother.

—1 John 4:16b-21

The two passages reflect separate, yet related, aspects of peer ministry:

● The passage from Luke gives us perspective on sharing our faith. To "lose our lives" means to give up our fear, insecurities and guilt, thus empowering us to reach out to others with "our very selves," the way God has created us. We grow by giving up our comfort zones and opening ourselves to God's direction.

● The passage from 1 John tells us in clear and beautiful terms the ultimate reason we reach out to others in peer ministry: God reached out to us first. Having experienced in our own lives God's power to heal us, comfort us and make us grow, we want to share it with others.

Peer ministry offers us opportunities to help hurting friends in our deeds and to share words of faith when appropriate.

*P*REPARATION

1. Prepare the meeting area for the training group:

warm, comfortable and not too large or too small. Obtain a chalkboard or newsprint pad and a hat. Photocopy a "Prayer of St. Francis of Assisi" handout for each person.

2. Read carefully through the session, becoming fully prepared and aware of its objectives and learning activities.

3. To help you think through the purpose and direction of this session, answer the following questions either in writing or in thought:

● What does the concept of "sharing faith" mean?

● How has God reached out to me in my faith journey? through friends? family? the Bible?

● With whom do I have difficulty sharing my faith? Why?

● What experiences have I had when I talked about faith in my home?

● What is my reaction to the cliché, "It's more important to show your faith than talk about it"?

● What are the differences between "caring" ministries and evangelism?

● What additional questions, points or examples can I use in making this lesson meaningful?

● Additional notes to myself:

Peer Ministry Training

OPENING

1. Pray. Open with a prayer by asking for God's guidance as participants seek to serve him.

2. It is important that all members participate in this session; therefore, you should act as the Observer. Ask for homework reports.

3. What is important about my Christian faith? Have students write on a piece of paper what they feel are the three most important aspects of their faith, and why.

You share first. Then go around the circle and ask each person to talk briefly about his or her most important aspects. Invite the group to ask the person questions to clarify what was shared. It is important that you narrow the topic sufficiently so that the student's belief is specific. Encourage the group to focus on their feelings about their beliefs.

SKILLS DEVELOPMENT

4. Sharing faith without using technical theological terms. Ask the group to identify common themes revealed during the time of sharing. Ask:

● What made it hard to express yourself?

● What were some common words or expressions?

Write these words on the board or newsprint. Then ask for other technical theological words people use in talking about faith.

Ask the group to identify which words are the most difficult to use and why. Which words are the most difficult to define? Take one or two of these and ask different members of the group to attempt to define them in common language.

5. Sharing faith with a critical person. Ask:

● Who are the most difficult kinds of people to talk with about your faith?

● What circumstances make it difficult to bring up your Christian faith?

● What do you fear the most about sharing your faith?

Ask each person to describe on a slip of paper a person with whom he or she finds difficulty in discussing the Christian faith. For example: a teacher who constantly ridicules religious faith; a friend who constantly swears in a deeply offensive manner; or a friend affiliated in a non-Christian religion. Put the slips in a hat. Then have each person draw one.

Divide the group into pairs. Have one member of the pair start by reading his or her slip of paper. The other partner is to assume the role of the person described. He or she should listen while the speaker practices talking about his or her faith. During this time the role player should also act as an observer by reflecting back to the speaker any impressions, misunderstandings or reactions that could affect the effectiveness of the faith-sharing.

Shift roles and repeat the process.

Some members may seem proficient at this and intimidate the others. After the activity ask the proficient people to relate how they acquired this skill. Ask them to describe how this proficiency has either helped or hindered them in learning how to share their faith.

*R*ESPONSE

Use the following questions for debriefing this activity and helping students respond to what they have experienced. Questions under the "Necessary transition questions" section should always be asked. The points you want to emphasize are summarized following the questions.

6. Necessary transition questions:

● What was most difficult for you in attempting to share your faith?

● Did the previous activity of sharing and talking about vocabulary help? Why or why not?

7. Examining the experience:
● Did you discover anything new in relation to your thoughts or feelings about your faith? Explain.
● What fears did you experience?
● How could you improve your abilities to share your faith more effectively?
8. Points to make about the learning activity:
● A beginning step in learning to express faith is to hear yourself do it.
● People often don't know the meaning of the theological terms they use.
● Sometimes people use theological terms or concepts that are foreign or meaningless to the unbeliever.
● Frequently our fear of others' reactions is unfounded. Other people often welcome the chance to discuss the Christian faith.
● One should remember to respect the rights and dignity of the other. Accusations build defense, not openness.
● Belief and faith are matters of the heart and emotions, and not simply matters of the head and reason. Speaking to the emotional needs of the other person is more effective.
● Arguments seldom convince or convert another, and they don't solidify relationships.

CLOSING

9. Since you were the Observer, give your report. Allow time for individuals to react to the observations.
10. Make me an instrument of your peace. Remind students that peer ministry is not preaching or using Bible passages to prove a point or forcing others to make decisions for Christ. Peer ministry is showing Christian love and service to hurting people.

Point out that words about Jesus and God have been trivialized and spoken in vain in our culture. Read the following parable:

"Once there was a boy who heard the preacher say God and Jesus a lot. His father said God when he was mad. His mother said Jesus when he got dirt on the carpet. Now he is old enough to say Jesus and God. He can say Jesus without even thinking. He can say God and not even mean it."

This parable reprinted from *"I" OPENER*, (Herbert Brokering) Copyright © 1974 by Concordia Publishing House. Used by permission.

Say: "What a difference actions make in 'speaking' our faith. As peer ministers, we share our faith by following Jesus' example."

Distribute a "Prayer of St. Francis of Assisi" handout to each person. Read the prayer aloud as a class.

Ask each person to share his or her response to the following sentence. You go first. "One way I can be an instrument of God's peace this coming week is . . ."

HOMEWORK ASSIGNMENT . . .

Approach a friend or acquaintance with whom you have never shared your faith, and begin a conversation with him or her about your faith.

HANDOUT:

Prayer of St. Francis of Assisi

*Lord, make me an instrument
  of your peace.
Where there is hatred, let me
  sow love;
where there is injury, pardon;
  where there is doubt, faith;
where there is despair, hope;
  where there is darkness, light;
and where there is sadness, joy.
O Divine Master, grant that
  I may not so much seek to be
consoled as to console; to be
  understood as to understand;
to be loved as to love; for it is
  in giving that we receive;
it is in pardoning that we are
  pardoned;
and it is in dying that we are
  born to eternal life.*

Simulating a Counseling Session

SESSION OBJECTIVES

Students will:

1. Learn to discriminate between significant and irrelevant information in understanding a counseling problem.

2. Develop and think of useful alternatives for solutions to problems.

3. Learn to identify the difference between presented problems and actual problems when working with a counselee.

4. Identify the important areas of information they need to help a counselee.

SCRIPTURE FOUNDATION

Do You Want to Get Well?

Some time later, Jesus went up to Jerusalem for a feast of the Jews. Now there is in Jerusalem near the Sheep Gate a pool, which in Aramaic is called Bethesda and which is surrounded by five covered colonnades. Here a great number of disabled people used to lie—the blind, the lame, the paralyzed. One who was there had been an invalid for thirty-eight years. When Jesus saw him lying there and learned that he had been in this condition for a long time, he asked him, "Do you want to get well?"

> *"Sir," the invalid replied, "I have no one to help*
> *me into the pool when the water is stirred. While I*
> *am trying to get in, someone else goes down ahead*
> *of me."*
> *Then Jesus said to him, "Get up! Pick up your mat*
> *and walk." At once the man was cured; he picked up*
> *his mat and walked.*
>
> *—John 5:1-9*

Many Bible passages deal with some aspect of counseling. The previous passage is particularly powerful in the context of counseling. The learning activity for this session stresses that a peer minister's task is to help others determine what they want to accomplish. "Do you want to get well?" is an appropriate question to ask another with problems.

Problems sometimes represent an unconscious flight from the responsibilities and difficulties of daily life. But the last thing we should try to do is assess the possible motivation behind other people's weaknesses. Sympathy can become a substitute for love. True counseling and love affirm. God wills us to be strong in him. It is for this reason he allows us to be confronted by our weakness. As counselors we help people face their weaknesses and find their strengths.

*P*REPARATION

1. Prepare the meeting area for the training group: warm, comfortable and not too large or too small. Obtain a chalkboard or newsprint pad. Photocopy a "Mary" handout and a "Checklist for Peer Ministers" handout for each person.

2. Read carefully through the session, becoming fully prepared and aware of its objectives and learning activities.

3. To help you think through the purpose and direction of this session, answer the following questions either in writing or in thought:

● What ideas do I have for alternatives to Mary's problems?

● What information would I give to a member of my group if I were to refer Mary to him or her? Why would I choose this information?

● How comfortable am I to let other people make their own decisions in choosing the "right" alternatives?

● When another person comes to me for help, do I find him or her a nuisance? Why or why not?

● How might a Christian counselor's methods differ from a non-Christian counselor's?

● What additional questions, points or examples can I use in making this lesson meaningful?

● Additional notes to myself:

Peer Ministry Training

OPENING

1. Pray. Open with a prayer by asking for God's guidance as participants seek to serve him.

2. Assign an Observer; and ask for homework reports.

3. Introduce the session topic. Tell students that they are beginning a transition from learning counseling skills to applying them. In this session, students will see what it's like to counsel another student.

Say that when asked to help another, a peer minister

will receive certain information about the counselee. Sometimes the information will be irrelevant. Sometimes there will be too much information. The peer minister needs to know the right information before he or she can be confident in counseling.

Sometimes what appears to be the problem is only the surface problem. Hurting people will usually present a "lesser" problem to see how another will listen. We have to ask ourselves if there is a deeper problem.

For example, a hurting person may approach or call you "just to talk." For a few moments he might say that he's keeping busy with sports, that the car is in the shop, that school is a hassle, etc. Depending on how the peer minister listens, the hurting person will then get to the reason he called: His girlfriend has dumped him.

As peer ministers we need to recognize the cries for help and the differences between the surface problems and the deeper ones.

*S*KILLS DEVELOPMENT

4. Counseling Mary. Divide the group into pairs. Give each pair a "Mary" handout. Say: "There is more information here than you normally would receive when asked to counsel a peer. In your pairs, read the 'Mary' profile. Then together attempt to answer the questions on the handout. I will ask for your opinions in the large group discussion."

When students have finished, bring the group together.

*R*ESPONSE

Use the following questions for debriefing this activity and helping students respond to what they have experienced. Questions under the "Necessary transition questions" section should always be asked. The points you want to emphasize are summarized following the questions.

5. Necessary transition questions:

● As pairs, share your answers to the "Mary" handout. (Many students are limited in their ideas of solutions or alternatives. Be prepared to make some suggestions, and perhaps write them on the board or newsprint.)

● Brainstorm what you think will happen to Mary if she takes no directed action in changing her life.

● Does she have a right not to take any action? Why or why not?

6. Examining the experience:

● What have you learned about the counseling process from this exercise?

● What are your ideas of what Mary might want to do to change her life? How could she do this? What kind of support would she need?

● What part of the counseling process seems the most difficult? Why?

7. Points to make about the learning activity:

● Often a counselee seeks help for an obvious or "safe" problem, while the actual problem is deeper and more serious.

● Exploring a person's values, strengths and weaknesses not only gives clues to the real problem, but also provides sources of alternatives for solutions.

● A counselor should start by encouraging the counselee to suggest alternatives. If the counselee doesn't have any ideas about alternatives, make some suggestions.

● Brainstorming ideas about alternatives helps peer ministers learn about possible solutions to problems.

● A peer minister's task is not to make sure the counselee commits to doing something. Rather, the important task is to help the counselee consider the consequences of any alternative he or she may be considering, including the alternative to continue what he or she is doing.

● Everyone has the freedom to fail, if he or she has been told the possible consequences.

● Regardless of a counselee's decision, the peer minister's primary responsibility is to give unconditional love and concern. Helping hurting people see Christ is our primary challenge.

Closing

8. Ask for the Observer's report. Allow time for individuals to react to the observations.

9. Referrals, confidentiality and review of peer ministry training. This is the last session of basic peer ministry training. Briefly cover the following three areas:

Referrals

● Some problems are beyond the abilities of peer ministers such as severe psychological disturbances, drug addiction, child abuse, venereal diseases, pregnancy and so on. These problems also have legal implications that can possibly affect peer ministers, their parents and the church.

● When in doubt, *always* refer hurting peers to professionals.

Confidentiality

● The success of an ongoing peer ministry program demands that confidentiality be maintained. Once a trust is broken, it is almost impossible to rebuild the counseling relationship.

● If the need arises for the peer minister to seek guidance for helping a peer, tell the students to follow these guidelines: Ask the counselee's permission to discuss the problem with you or another professional. If the peer's physical well-being is at risk, the peer minister must tell you or another appropriate professional about the situation.

Review of peer ministry training

● Briefly review the content of the basic training and ask students to ask any questions and share what was most meaningful to them.

● You may either pass out or mail the "Checklist for Peer Ministers" handout for the students to keep.

10. Peer ministry commissioning. If you choose to do the six advanced sessions, save this commissioning and use it after Advanced Session 6.

You may wish to use candlelight for this commissioning. Say: "This is the last session of our peer ministry training program. We have worked on the skills of listening, questioning and reading non-verbal communication. We have looked at decision-making, values and sharing our faith. For centuries the church has commissioned those who have been willing to go into the world and show God's grace by serving others."

Stand in a circle. Ask one of the students to come to the center of the group. Ask the other students to lay a hand on the person's shoulders. Ask students to bow their heads as you pray: "Lord, we thank you for Sharon and her willingness to serve you by loving and listening to others in her life. Fill Sharon with your Holy Spirit to reach out to peers in Christian love and service. We pray this in the name of Christ, who gives us power and courage, amen."

Ask each student to hug the person just prayed for. Repeat the process for everyone in the group. Close with the Lord's Prayer.

HOMEWORK ASSIGNMENT . . .

Ask students to think about the most significant problem of one of their family members or friends. What could they do to help? Have the students put into practice what they have learned and counsel a person in need. Although this assignment will not be discussed, completing it is vital.

HANDOUTS:

Mary

Mary, age 15, is an extremely intelligent and creative girl. In junior high and in her sophomore year, she received honors and was placed in advanced classes. Teachers praised her for her creative writing, and she did some outstanding artwork, particularly with watercolors. She loved to do portraits.

In junior high, Mary got all A's and B's. But during her sophomore year a dramatic change took place. She skipped school frequently, failed to turn in assignments, was likely to be suspended and eventually withdrew from school to attend a private school. As a result, she failed all her classes except painting and P.E., and only earned one unit of credit in the 10th-grade.

She didn't like the private school either, so she returned to her former high school, and now wants to take classes with her classmates, although they are a year ahead of her. But she still seems lost, and she questions the purpose of school, going on to college, society's values, the church, etc.

Mary has an older brother who lives at home, but is attending a nearby state college as a freshman. Her father

(continued on next page)

is a librarian at this college, earning $26,000 per year. Mary's mother does office work at a nearby private university. She makes $14,000 per year. Both parents are college graduates.

After school, Mary meets with close friends for "discussions" about life, society and personal problems. Sometimes she stays up all night, either painting or writing poetry. She occasionally dates college and graduate students, and is allowed a lot of freedom as to what she does. Mary attends church off and on, and came a couple of times to youth group. She believes in God, but says she is not a goody-goody.

She has no future plans. She is under a lot of pressure from her parents to go to college. Since she is an avid reader, she has learned a great deal, and she often realizes she is more educated than many of her peers, and even some of her teachers. She is not opposed to learning, but to having to meet all the requirements of a formal education. The tension at home is increasing and adding to her problems of what to do with her life, where to go, and even who she is as a person.

Counseling questions:
● What kind of a person is described?
● What does Mary value? What doesn't she value?
● What are her strengths? weaknesses?
● What do you feel is Mary's most important problem?
● What additional information would you like to have about Mary?
● Where might she find help?
● What alternatives might you suggest to help Mary resolve the prime problem?
● How can you reach out to Mary in Christian love and concern?

Checklist for Peer Ministers

A peer minister:

1. Is a warm, genuine and empathic person.

2. Listens for the meaning behind words.

3. Helps a peer clarify a confusing concern, sorting out the "safe" problem from the real one.

4. Allows the peer to talk about this deeper, more "risky" problem.

5. Helps the peer clarify personal values.

6. Explores alternatives and the potential consequences or outcomes of each alternative.

7. Is able to ask open and feeling-level questions when appropriate.

8. Makes observations and checks out assumptions based on observation.

9. Realizes that not all problems can be solved and not all peers want to be helped.

10. Knows when to refer a peer to a professional adult.

11. Keeps in mind the primary purpose of peer ministry: To love God by loving one's neighbor as oneself.

A peer minister does not:

1. Tell peers what to do.

2. Try to bandage a problem with cheap sympathy.

3. Talk mainly about oneself.

4. Encourage dependency.

5. Put peers down.

6. Gossip about what was said in a counseling session or in any other way violate confidentiality.

7. Act as if he or she is superior to peers.

8. Expect all problems to be solved easily and quickly.

9. Work with a peer whose problem is not appropriate for a peer minister.

Assertive Communication

SESSION OBJECTIVES

Students will:

1. Learn how to express personal rights and desires, especially in peer pressure situations.

2. Distinguish assertiveness from three other types of responses.

3. Practice using "I" messages and other ways to communicate effectively.

SCRIPTURE FOUNDATION

The Tongue of the Wise

A gentle answer turns away wrath,
  but a harsh word stirs up anger.

The tongue of the wise commends knowledge,
  but the mouth of the fool gushes folly.

The tongue that brings healing is a tree of life,
  but a deceitful tongue crushes the spirit.

A hot-tempered man stirs up dissension,
  but a patient man calms a quarrel.
                    —Proverbs 15:1-2, 4, 18

These proverbs set the tone for this session. A gentle response to anger softens the heart and tongue of the attacker or accuser. Arguing feeds disagreement and bad tempers. Patience and humility not only resolve discord, but are pleasing to the Lord.

Full understanding of these concepts should help peer ministers understand the attitude they will need in being direct with others. Having the right attitude is more important than using the right words. The messages of these passages suggest that the Lord expects us to show love, kindness, patience and humility toward others even when we are wronged. A Christian who has these qualities is not easily put down.

When instructing Titus about dealing with others, Paul said: "In everything set them an example by doing what is good. In your teaching show integrity, seriousness and soundness of speech that cannot be condemned . . ." (Titus 2:7-8).

He told Timothy to "set an example for the believers in speech, in life, in love, in faith and in purity" (1 Timothy 4:12).

A careless action of speech, reference or slur makes it easier for another to follow suit. Speaking directly and showing kindness, courtesy and respect also make it easier for another to follow suit.

We are not perfect. We must not allow a self-righteousness to prevail but a love that arises from our acceptance of our own sinful and forgiven condition.

We must also learn to wait out some situations, to create opportunities in other situations, and to pray for the wisdom and courage to know what to do.

*P*REPARATION

1. Prepare the meeting area for the training group: warm, comfortable and not too large or too small.

Obtain a chalkboard or newsprint pad, paper and pencils. Make two copies of the "Situation A" handout and the "Situation B" handout.

2. Read carefully through the session, becoming fully prepared and aware of its objectives and learning activities.

3. To help you think through the purpose and direction of this session, answer the following questions either in writing or in thought:

● How do I define assertiveness? Is it different from my definition of humility? pride? passivity?

● How difficult is it for me to deal with people who act aggressively?

● How do I feel when Christians aren't easy to get along with? How about non-Christians?

● How do I feel when I am assertive with others, yet don't succeed in changing their attitudes?

● What additional questions, points or examples can I use in making this lesson meaningful?

● Additional notes to myself:

Peer Ministry Training

*O*PENING

1. Pray. Open with a prayer by asking for God's guidance as participants seek to serve him.

2. Assign an Observer.

3. What does "peer pressure" mean? Say: "What do you think of when you hear the words 'peer pressure'? Describe a recent situation in which you felt peer pressure. Tell about either a positive or a negative experience. Describe how you handled the pressure in that particular situation."

Ask the students to find a partner and share their situations and how they handled them. Then ask the pairs to discuss: Which makes peer pressure more difficult to handle—the *person* who pressures, or the *action* you are pressured to do? Why?

Skills Development

4. Role-work demonstration. Tell students that you will demonstrate four different ways to respond to a typical pressure situation. Ask a volunteer to take the part of a student making a "pressured" request. The situation is this:

It is the day before an important social studies test. A member of the class has been cutting frequently, even though he knows that this test will include many questions from class lectures. On the way out of class, this student asks if he can borrow your notes for the night. You don't know this classmate well, and you haven't had a chance to study your notes yourself. You really don't want to lend your notes.

The student taking the role of the one asking for the notes can say or do anything he chooses to get the notes from you. You must exaggerate each of the four responses to make the differences between them clear. After each of the brief demonstrations, ask for reactions from the group members. Following their comments, identify the kind of response you were modeling such as "Passive," "Aggressive," etc. For example:

Student to you: "Hi! May I borrow your notes for the social studies test tomorrow?"

Passive: "Yes . . . Ah, I guess you can have them."

(Look down; shrug, use a weak tone of voice and sound a little depressed.)

Passive-Aggressive: "Gee . . . Ah . . . Well, I guess you can have them, but it'll really make it difficult for me. I'll probably flunk . . . but you can have them." (Use a tone of sarcasm or restrained anger. Say what you can to make him feel guilty for accepting your notes.)

Aggressive: "You jerk! How dumb do you think I am? Do you think I'm going to give you my notes after you've been cutting school and I've been in class slaving away taking those notes? Of course I'm not going to lend you the notes and I hope you get what you deserve in that test tomorrow." (Look and act angry and incensed, stand erect, use strong eye contact and a loud voice while jabbing your finger at the student.)

Assertive: "No, I'm sorry, but you can't. I need them myself. I've been working hard to get a good grade in that class and have planned to use them tonight to prepare for the test." (Look directly at the student, use a firm tone of voice without any anger or apology in it, and stand up straight but not rigid.)

After the demonstration, have the group members discuss what they observed. Help them gain a clearer understanding of the differences in these approaches. Ask:

● Which of the four responses do you feel was most effective? Why?

● Which one do you use most frequently? Why?

● Which one is the hardest to use? Why?

Using what they have said, explain why people use these approaches. For example, some people may lack confidence in themselves, lack a sense of strong values, desire not to hurt others and so on. Suggested definitions of the four responses are the following:

Passive: Never asking for or expressing your rights

and feelings, being afraid to express desires for fear you won't be liked, putting yourself down, always giving in to others, saying yes when you don't want to, letting people walk all over you.

Passive-Aggressive: Appearing to go along with the other's wishes or desires but making him or her pay for it in some way, saying one thing but meaning another, hiding feelings that come out in different ways, trying to make another feel guilty about the request.

Aggressive: Handling a situation by attacking the other, getting angry, using put-downs to get your way, disregarding the other's feelings or desires, being pushy, always needing to win or be right.

Assertive: Honestly expressing your rights and desires, firmly and kindly. Not letting yourself be pushed around, and not attempting to push others around. Expressing your own plans, desires or decisions simply but clearly.

In discussing the "Assertive" response, which you are trying to teach, make the distinction between assertiveness and selfishness. You are not teaching that one should get his or her way all the time. Sometimes a person needs to sacrifice what he or she wants in order for the group to get along, or as a kindness to another. But when something is important, and one feels a right to express a desire, then the skill to say no or express one's wishes is necessary. The basis of this is self-respect and the right to ask others for respect.

5. Assertive communication practice. Ask two students to volunteer to practice being assertive in a social relationship situation. Give each a copy of the "Situation A" handout. Ask one student to act as the dance chairperson and the other to respond as the pressured student. After they have done this, ask the class to give feedback as to how successful the assertive person was and to suggest any alternative approaches that might have been used.

Follow this with the "Situation B" handout, asking for two other volunteers.

RESPONSE

Use the following questions for debriefing this activity and helping students respond to what they have experienced. Questions under the "Necessary transition questions" section should always be asked. The points you want to emphasize are summarized following the questions.

6. Necessary transition questions:

For the student who was pressured:

● How did you feel about how you handled this?

● What made it hard?

● What feelings did you have about the other person and yourself?

For the student who made the request:

● What was your reaction to what your partner said?

● How could you have exerted more pressure on him or her?

7. Examining the experience:

● Why are you sometimes afraid to say no?

● How do you feel when someone tries to get you to do something by making you feel guilty?

● What do your friends do when they are angry but won't say anything?

● What happens when you and your friends *do* honestly share feelings and thoughts?

● How do you react to pushy and aggressive people?

● How can you show Christian love and concern in an assertive way?

8. Points to make about the learning activity:

● Assertiveness is being honest with another, without devaluing that person. The other person may not like to hear what you say, but he or she may respect you for saying it. He or she can accept your refusal without feeling attacked or disgraced. This tends to build trust in relationships.

● By not having to lie or make excuses, you can use direct eye contact.

● By not getting angry or attacking another, you feel better about yourself.

● Since your intent is to stand up for yourself, you do not have to seek revenge or hurt the other.

● Your tone of voice and volume are not apologetic or angry, and therefore, are assets in getting the other to listen and to accept what you say.

● You only have control over yourself. The greatest gift you can give to another is honesty, care and kindness. If the other person chooses not to accept your message in this way, at least you have not intentionally hurt him or her.

CLOSING

9. Ask for the Observer's report. Allow time for individuals to react to the observations.

10. Setting an example for the believers in speech. Affirm the students' power to use speech in positive, servant-oriented ways. Say: "There is nothing more important in peer ministry than caring communication. How you listen to people and what you say have power. It's your choice how you will use this power. James says: 'With the tongue we praise our Lord and Father, and with it we curse men, who have been made in God's likeness. Out of the same mouth come praise and cursing. My brothers, this should not be' (James 3:9-10).

"In peer ministry, you will be tempted to talk a lot.

Resist that temptation! Peer ministry is *not* giving advice, rescuing, preaching, 'you' statements, judging, telling others what they 'should' do, etc. Peer ministry is letting the other person do most of the talking, while you do the listening and understanding.''

Divide into pairs. For the closing prayer, ask students to share their concerns and pray for each other using "I" messages. For example: "I want to thank God for my family." "I ask for God's guidance in a tough decision I have to make about school." Encourage students to continue to pray for their partners during the coming week.

*H*OMEWORK ASSIGNMENT . . .

Ask students to apply the "Assertive" response to a situation this week in which they are asked or pressured to do something against their wishes, values or sense of what is appropriate.

HANDOUTS:

Situation A

You just bought four albums you've wanted for a long time with money you earned yourself. You take very good care of your albums and are proud of them. The dance chairperson comes up to you in the hall. He or she says: "Hey, I hear you have some great new albums! Bring them to the dance on Friday night, okay? All of the albums we've been using are scratched and wrecked."

Situation B

Your neighbor comes over to ask you to babysit on Friday night. You have had bad experiences babysitting the neighbor's children in the past. They were undisciplined and hard to handle. Although you don't have any special plans, you don't want to babysit. He or she says: "I would really appreciate it if you would babysit Friday night. It would really help me out a lot."

*F*amily Relationships

*S*ESSION OBJECTIVES

Students will:

1. Learn how it feels to have family problems.

2. Learn how to minister to someone with family problems.

*S*CRIPTURE FOUNDATION

The Parable of the Prodigal Son

Jesus continued: "There was a man who had two sons. The younger one said to his father, 'Father, give me my share of the estate.' So he divided his property between them.

"Not long after that, the younger son got together all he had, set off for a distant country and there squandered his wealth in wild living. After he had spent everything, there was a severe famine in that whole country, and he began to be in need. So he went and hired himself out to a citizen of that country, who sent him to his fields to feed pigs. He longed to fill his stomach with the pods that the pigs were eating, but no one gave him anything.

"When he came to his senses, he said, 'How many of my father's hired men have food to spare, and here I am starving to death! I will set out and go back to my father and say to him: Father, I have sinned against heaven and against you. I am no longer worthy to be called your son; make me like one of your hired men.' So he got up and went to his

father.

"But while he was still a long way off, his father saw him and was filled with compassion for him; he ran to his son, threw his arms around him and kissed him.

"The son said to him, 'Father, I have sinned against heaven and against you. I am no longer worthy to be called your son.'

"But the father said to his servants, 'Quick! Bring the best robe and put it on him. Put a ring on his finger and sandals on his feet. Bring the fattened calf and kill it. Let's have a feast and celebrate. For this son of mine was dead and is alive again; he was lost and is found.' So they began to celebrate.

"Meanwhile, the older son was in the field. When he came near the house, he heard music and dancing. So he called one of the servants and asked him what was going on. 'Your brother has come,' he replied, 'and your father has killed the fattened calf because he has him back safe and sound.'

"The older brother became angry and refused to go in. So his father went out and pleaded with him. But he answered his father, 'Look! All these years I've been slaving for you and never disobeyed your orders. Yet you never gave me even a young goat so I could celebrate with my friends. But when this son of yours who has squandered your property with prostitutes comes home, you kill the fattened calf for him!'

" 'My son,' the father said, 'you are always with me, and everything I have is yours. But we had to celebrate and be glad, because this brother of yours was dead and is alive again; he was lost and is found.' "

—Luke 15:11-32

The parable of the prodigal son shows many aspects of family problems as well as solutions. Rebellion against family constraints leads to a variety of actions. Often a child doesn't have the strength to ask for forgiveness and return to the family fold. The prodigal son had no true understanding of the depth of his

father's love. How many of us misread the love from
our family members? Do we believe we are loved?
This parable illustrates some of these family issues
and solutions. This parable also is a story of two
prodigals. The father lost both of his sons, one in the
far country, and the other in a morass of self-righteous
resentment.

Two stories from Genesis illustrate other emotions
that enter into family strife: favoritism and jealousy.
Isaac favored Esau—but Rebekah favored Jacob (Genesis 25:19-34). Cain's murder of his brother Abel
(Genesis 4:2-8) illustrates the power of jealousy to
dominate one's whole being.

Resentment, jealousy, anger and guilt are problems
of the heart. It is difficult to resolve such problems
with human counseling. The most important ther-
apeutic concepts in the Bible are God's grace, love
and forgiveness. True forgiveness can dissolve guilt.
True love can overcome resentment.

The Holy Spirit changes our hearts and gives us the
desire and ability to love and forgive our family
members.

*P*REPARATION

1. Prepare the meeting area for the training group:
warm, comfortable and not too large or too small.
Obtain a chalkboard or newsprint pad.

2. Read carefully through the session, becoming
fully prepared and aware of its objectives and learning activities.

3. To help you think through the purpose and
direction of this session, answer the following questions either in writing or in thought:

● What are characteristics of a Christian family?

● How does my family resolve difficulties in ways
that differ from non-Christian families?

● How often do I attempt a Christian approach to our family conflicts?

● Why is it hard to forgive? What do I gain or lose by forgiving a family member?

● Why is it sometimes difficult to ask for forgiveness from a family member?

● What additional questions, points or examples can I use in making this lesson meaningful?

● Additional notes to myself:

Peer Ministry Training

OPENING

1. Pray. Open with a prayer by asking for God's guidance as participants seek to serve him.

2. Assign an Observer; and ask for homework reports.

3. Introduce the topic of family relationships. Ask the students, one at a time, to share with the class what a typical evening is like in their homes. On the board or on newsprint, write the following questions and others you might add:

● If someone were to surprise you tonight and appear at your home during the dinner hour, what would he or she see going on?

● Who would be there?

● Would the television be on?

● What would the table look like?

● What would conversations center on and who

would do most of the talking?
- Would you be enjoying yourself?
- What happens after dinner? homework? TV viewing? family devotions?

After all have shared, ask the class:
- What are some positive family experiences?
- What are some common family problems?
- How well do most families deal with these problems?

Possible examples of family problems are the following:
- Lack of communication with parents.
- Overly rigid rules.
- Arguments among parents.
- Living with only one parent.
- Pain and struggle because of a separation or divorce.
- Silence among family members.
- Sibling rivalry.
- Parents distrust children and dislike their friends.
- Parents rarely home.
- Stress caused by death, economic change, illness, alcoholism, and extended relatives or others sharing home space.

SKILLS DEVELOPMENT

4. Role working a family problem. If a student has indicated deep feelings about a particular problem, ask this student if he or she is willing to have another peer minister attempt to help him or her. If he or she agrees, ask for a volunteer to take the role of peer minister.

If no one indicates a problem, select a common problem mentioned and ask a student to take the role of someone having that problem. Ask another to take the role of peer minister.

Ask these two to practice this situation in front of the group. Ask the other group members to observe the counseling session carefully.

Stop the role working when the peer minister needs help or when the content is repeated.

Ask the peer minister how he or she felt about working through the problem. What skills seemed successful? What skills need improvement?

Ask the counselee how he or she felt about the peer minister's help. What seemed most effective?

Ask the group for reactions, comments and suggestions.

5. Practice peer ministry in pairs. Divide the group into pairs. Have one member in each pair share a genuine family concern. The other partner should practice counseling with him or her about this problem.

After 15 minutes, ask pairs to shift roles. Then come back together in the large group.

*R*ESPONSE

Use the following questions for debriefing this activity and helping students respond to what they have experienced. Questions under the "Necessary transition questions" section should always be asked. The points you want to emphasize are summarized following the questions.

6. Necessary transition questions:

● Did the peer minister seem to understand the problem? Explain.

● Did the peer minister ask clarifying questions? Explain.

● Did the troubled student find the peer minister helpful? In what ways?

7. Examining the experience:

● Did the peer minister attempt to give advice?

Was this effective?
- What suggestions or alternatives were given?
- Which ones seemed most useful?
- Did the counselee feel he or she was being judged by the peer minister? Explain.
- What did you learn from this experience?

8. Points to make about the learning activity:
- Many young people will feel frustrated because they didn't know what to do to help. Discuss their frustrations in the large group and brainstorm possible alternatives to help resolve family problems.
- Discuss how the students can contribute to better family relationships. The following questions will help students begin thinking about their influence over family life and situations:
- How would you describe your actions toward your family?
- How do you feel you contribute to your family? What are the most important ways you contribute?
- How does your family contribute to you? Do they know that you appreciate this?
- What is the difference between a Christian and a non-Christian family? How can you apply your faith in your own family?
- Who do you feel needs you the most in your family? What does he or she need from you?
- What do you need most from your family? From which particular members?
- What do you do when you notice that a member of your family is upset or has had a bad day? In what ways could you help when this happens?
- How do you act when you are upset? How does this behavior affect the family?
- What do you do when a family member hurts your feelings?
- What do you lose or gain by fighting back when a family member picks on you?

● How could you help your family be more caring in their communication with one another?

● How do you feel your parents would describe you? Is this different from how you would describe yourself?

● What would you like to change the most in your family? What are possible ways you could do this?

CLOSING

9. Ask for the Observer's report. Allow time for individuals to react to the observations.

10. We are the family of God. Have the students look at the likeness of their families to the family of God, especially the "brothers and sisters" in the training group.

Say: "God has called us family. Jesus often referred to his followers as brothers and sisters. We should take this seriously, that our true family is God's family. It's important to treat our Christian brothers and sisters with family love. And just as in our own families, there will be hassles, disputes and sin. As peer ministers, we need to take the first step in forgiving and attempting reconciliation."

Read Jesus' words in Matthew 5:23-24:

"Therefore, if you are offering your gift at the altar and there remember that your brother has something against you, leave your gift there in front of the altar. First go and be reconciled to your brother; then come and offer your gift."

Ask the students each to close their eyes and visualize the face of someone with whom they need to reconcile a problem. It might be someone in the training group, a friend or a family member. Ask them to imagine telling that person about their anger and pain. Then ask the students each to say: "I forgive you. Thank you, God."

Pray: "Lord, we thank you for giving us the power to forgive, for healing the hurts we don't deserve, and for forgiving us when we fall short. In Jesus' name, amen."

HOMEWORK ASSIGNMENT . . .

Ask students to work on one problem within their families this week. Make sure they work on a *realistic* problem. For example, a student can't realistically work on "getting my parents back together." He or she can, however, work on communicating more effectively with a parent about a chore or curfew.

*P*eer Relationships

*S*ESSION OBJECTIVES

Students will:

1. Learn how it feels to have problems with friends and other peers.

2. Learn how to minister to a peer having friendship problems.

*S*CRIPTURE FOUNDATION

I Have Called You Friends

"My command is this: Love each other as I have loved you. Greater love has no one than this, that he lay down his life for his friends. You are my friends if you do what I command. I no longer call you servants, because a servant does not know his master's business. Instead, I have called you friends, for everything that I learned from my Father I have made known to you. You did not choose me, but I chose you and appointed you to go and bear fruit—fruit that will last. Then the Father will give you whatever you ask in my name. This is my command: Love each other."

—John 15:12-17

Many problems in peer relationships can be traced to an individual's lack of feeling unconditionally loved. This in turn affects the individual's understanding of true friendship. Behaviors such as shyness, rivalry and cliques substitute real friendship.

Shyness is self-depreciation. Competitiveness and ambition show a need to prove oneself, to have a sense of worth. Cliques and put-downs frequently rise from insecurity. But when people experience love and acceptance, their ability to love others and themselves grows stronger and their insecurities and problems within relationships fade.

Jesus said we are to love as he has loved us. Christians grow to love others as they repeatedly realize the unfailing love of Christ. But a relationship with Christ is not only personal. It means serving others and giving of ourselves.

This session, more than most of the other sessions, deals with the prime purpose of peer ministry: learning to care for others as a response to our faith in God.

In the learning activity, some students will fear talking about real problems they have with peers. That's okay, because the peers with whom they will minister will probably have similar fears. Empathy is a great asset in peer counseling situations.

*P*REPARATION

1. Prepare the meeting area for the training group: warm, comfortable and not too large or too small. Obtain a chalkboard or newsprint pad. Photocopy an "I Need a Friend" handout for each person.

2. Read carefully through the session, becoming fully prepared and aware of its objectives and learning activities.

3. To help you think through the purpose and direction of this session, answer the following questions either in writing or in thought:

● How have I experienced God's love?

● What signs do I look for as proof of God's love?

- Who loves me?
- Who do I find hard to love?
- How do I encourage the youth group to be an environment for love?
- Am I hard to love? Why?
- What do I stand to gain or lose by loving another?
- What additional questions, points or examples can I use in making this lesson meaningful?
- Additional notes to myself:

Peer Ministry Training

OPENING

1. Pray. Open with a prayer by asking for God's guidance as participants seek to serve him.

2. Assign an Observer; and ask for homework reports.

3. Introduce the topic. The most common problem students will be working with in their roles as peer ministers is that of peer relationships. A problem may result from rejection, extreme shyness, negative school atmosphere or even a complacent Christian youth group. Wherever they go, they will have peer relationship problems.

For these reasons the focus of this session is dual. It deals with helping others acquire the kinds of friends they want; and how to contribute to making the youth group more positive, friendly and Christlike.

4. Ask about peer relationship problems. Tell students to think about their past school and church life. Ask:

● What were some of your most difficult times with your peers?

● What made these times difficult?

● How have these times affected your relationships with your peers now?

Using what students have shared, lead the group to identify common problems that occur frequently. Sort out those that relate to the school or youth group environment (such as cliques) and those that relate to personal characteristics (such as shyness). Could the same problems happen to other students in their schools or youth groups? Discuss the conditions of the environment first, then discuss personal characteristics and counseling.

School or youth group environment:

● How does one become a "star" in your school? Is it through athletics? student government? music?

● How does one learn how to "make it" in your school? Is becoming a "star" under your control, or does it depend on others? Are there equal opportunities for both girls and boys?

● Who are the unpopular students in your school? Do they have something in common, or is it all a matter of individual behavior? Who makes them unpopular?

● Are there cliques in your school? Which are the most prestigious? How does one get into them? How do they hurt others? Would you like a school without cliques? Why?

● Do you feel that the popularity system has a positive or a negative influence on the social lives of the entire student body? Why?

● What would you like to change the most about your school in terms of social relationships? How could teachers help?

● How important is appearance in your school—the clothes you wear, the way you look, and sloppiness versus neatness?

● What messages do people give through their appearances? What messages are you giving today with the clothes you are wearing and how you look?

Personal characteristics:

● What makes it difficult to be friendly?

● What is shyness?

● What creates social confidence? Is social confidence good or bad? Explain.

● What do you or others do to get attention from peers?

● What kinds of students do you admire?

● What qualities or characteristics do you have that would make you a desirable friend?

● What is the difference between friendliness and friendship?

● What are some important ingredients of friendship?

● What have you done to make your school or youth group a friendlier place?

● What qualities or skills would you like to learn to be a more effective friend?

● How might you as an individual, or as a peer minister, show friendship to some lonely, unattractive students in your school or youth group?

*S*KILLS DEVELOPMENT

5. Role working positive peer relationships and counseling. Three different situations are suggested to practice dealing with peer relationships. Decide which one to use based on what has come out in the discussion or on the group's needs. Another option is to have pairs counsel each other about actual problems they are experiencing in their peer relationships.

● *Peer ministry with a student who is shy or has no friends.* Select someone to take the role of a shy person. Review the kinds of behaviors and feelings of such a person based on the discussion. Select another student to be the peer minister.

Ask the pair to role work the situation in front of the group. Or you can divide the group into pairs to go through this activity.

● *Peer ministry with a student who is unpopular.* Often a student is unpopular for legitimate reasons. His or her behavior or actions turn peers off. This person may not know how to behave in different ways or may need some constructive feedback about what effect his or her behavior has on others.

Peer ministers need help in learning how to talk to another about these matters. Sometimes students in the group have demonstrated some of these negative behaviors. If so, an actual counseling situation could be enacted. It would be better to do this in pairs, privately, rather than in front of the group.

● *Peer ministry in a group.* Sometimes a thoughtful peer minister will want to help his or her own group of friends be more kind and thoughtful to another student. It takes skill and courage to attempt to change the actions and attitudes of one's own group.

To role work this situation, divide students into groups of three or four. Ask each group to create its own social setting. Have each person take a turn at being the peer minister talking to his or her friends.

RESPONSE

Use the following questions for debriefing this activity and helping students respond to what they have experienced. Questions under the "Necessary transition questions'' section should always be asked. The points you want to emphasize are summarized following the questions.

6. Necessary transition questions:

● Did the peer minister seem to understand the problem? Explain.

● Did the peer minister ask clarifying questions? Explain.

● Did the troubled student find the peer minister helpful? In what ways?

7. Examining the experience:

● Did the peer minister attempt to give advice? Was this effective?

● What suggestions or alternatives were given?

● Which ones seemed most useful?

● Did the counselee feel he or she was being judged by the peer minister? Explain.

● What did you learn from this experience?

8. Points to make about the learning activity:

● Peer influence can be either negative or positive.

● Students can have a positive influence over others if they are willing to try. Encourage and praise participants for their efforts.

● Some students might express fears about the possibility of rejection. Point out that a hurting person will often initially reject a caring person's attempts to minister. This initial rejection tests whether the peer minister truly cares.

● Some students might express feelings of inadequacy. But peer ministers are not problem solvers or advice givers. Their first priority is to listen instead of speak.

Closing

9. Ask for the Observer's report. Allow time for individuals to react to the observations.

10. We need a friend. Have students look at their need for friends and how peer ministry is being the kind of friend we would like to have.

Distribute an "I Need a Friend" handout to each person. Ask for a volunteer to read the "Leader" part. Then proceed with the responsive reading.

After the reading, gather in a circle. Have each student turn to the person next to him or her and do an open-eyed prayer. Stress that students should look at each other while they're praying. Eye contact brings us closer to God and each other. Students should also take turns thanking God for the friendship qualities they see in the other person.

*H*OMEWORK ASSIGNMENT . . .

Discuss what students could do to make the youth group a friendlier place. Urge them to start doing this during the next week. Tell them you will ask for a report on what they have done.

HANDOUT:

I Need a Friend

Leader: All by myself I can eat a sandwich
Class: But I need a friend to have a picnic.

Leader: All by myself I can run
Class: But I need a friend to race.

Leader: All by myself I can skin my knee
Class: But I need a friend to feel sorry.

Leader: All by myself I can know a secret
Class: But I need a friend to whisper it to.

Leader: All by myself I can guess a riddle
Class: But I need a friend to tell it.

Leader: All by myself I can dream a story
Class: But I need a friend to listen to it.

Leader: All by myself I can play alone
Class: But I need a friend for sharing.

Substance Abuse

SESSION OBJECTIVES

Students will:

1. Learn where they stand in their values toward substance abuse and health.

2. Learn how to minister to someone with a substance abuse problem.

SCRIPTURE FOUNDATION

There Is Nothing Concealed

Jesus began to speak first to his disciples, saying: "Be on your guard against the yeast of the Pharisees, which is hypocrisy. There is nothing concealed that will not be disclosed, or hidden that will not be made known. What you have said in the dark will be heard in the daylight, and what you have whispered in the ear in the inner rooms will be proclaimed from the roofs."

—Luke 12:1b-3

I Will Not Be Mastered by Anything

"Everything is permissible for me"—but not everything is beneficial. "Everything is permissible for me"—but I will not be mastered by anything.

Do you not know that your body is a temple of the Holy Spirit, who is in you, whom you have received from God? You are not your own; you were bought at a price. Therefore honor God with your body.

—1 Corinthians 6:12, 19-20

Jesus tried hard to disassociate himself from the Pharisees and to warn his disciples against their influence. Groups that try to entice us into substance use are like the Pharisees. They place so much importance on social acceptance and outward appearance that they neglect what really matters in life, that is, a relationship with God. As a result, substance abusers live a life of self-deception.

Behind this self-deception is a desire to escape. In looking at life, substance abusers fear rejection, loneliness, failure and personal risks. They can't see that it's safer to face problems honestly. Ill use of the body is often a result of trying to escape problems and tough times.

By realizing our bodies are temples of the Holy Spirit, we can escape the snare of negative influence. We can learn to honor and discipline both our bodies and our emotions. We can clear ourselves of the habits that destroy our minds and bodies.

Remember that peer ministers are just as vulnerable to being drawn into substance abuse as any other student. One common form of substance abuse is drug abuse. A recent Gallup Youth Survey found that teenagers think the biggest problem facing people their age is drug abuse. For these reasons, this session focuses on helping students decide their own values about drug abuse. This session also alerts students to the underlying causes and behaviors leading to drug abuse.

*P*REPARATION

1. Prepare the meeting area for the training group: warm, comfortable and not too large or too small. Obtain a chalkboard or newsprint pad, and pencils. Photocopy an "Anonymous Quiz" handout for each person.

2. Read carefully through the session, becoming fully prepared and aware of its objectives and learning activities.

3. To help you think through the purpose and direction of this session, answer the following questions either in writing or in thought:

● Do I use drugs? (Include alcohol, since it is a drug.) Why do I use them? How do I misuse them? Is there a legitimate difference between my use and adolescents' use?

● Think about my use of other substances: chocolate, food, caffeine, sugar, tobacco, etc. Is my use of these legitimate?

● Does my church abuse food? Do coffee and doughnut times at church on Sunday mornings convey a positive message about substance use?

● Am I mastered by anything? my work? my dead-end relationships? my misuse of time?

● What additional questions, points or examples can I use in making this lesson meaningful?

● Additional notes to myself:

4. You are a model to your students. Young people are vulnerable. If you do not believe you can introduce positive values on substance use, we suggest you not use this session.

5. Be prepared to answer any questions students may ask about your use of substances. If you wish you didn't use certain substances such as beer or junk food, acknowledge this. If you practice some ways to control your behavior in these areas, share them with the group.

6. Consider whether you want to have peer ministers counsel with someone who has a severe drug problem. This complicated problem is difficult even for professionals. But students can be effective in getting drug users to seek help for themselves, even though the peer ministers may not do the counseling.

Peer Ministry Training

OPENING

1. Pray. Open with a prayer by asking for God's guidance as participants seek to serve him.

2. Assign an Observer; and ask for homework reports.

3. Pass out copies of the "Anonymous Quiz." Have students complete the quiz, without signing their names. Tell them that they will study the findings as a group.

After everyone has finished, collect and redistribute the quizzes to the group. Discuss each statement, asking the students to raise their hands if the sheet they are holding has a checkmark in either the "Yes" or "No" column.

After a few of the statements, ask volunteers to share reactions to the quiz. Do they agree with the quiz responses? Why or why not?

Explain that this session will deal with the issue of substance abuse. Substance abuse means more than illegal drug use. It means abuse of alcohol, caffeine, chocolate—any substance that can be taken internally which will alter a person's physical or emotional state. This session will clarify values regarding substance abuse and train students to reach out to substance abusers. The main focus will be on drug abuse since it is a common form of abuse, and teenagers view it as the biggest problem facing their peers today.

4. Bring the discussion "home." Ask:

● If I were a new student in your school, what sort of drug use might I find when I go to my first party?

● What kinds of students would be using these drugs?

● What kinds of students would not be using drugs?

● Where would I go if I wanted to obtain drugs?

● Would I have a difficult time finding a close group of friends who don't use drugs? Why or why not?

SKILLS DEVELOPMENT

5. Build a profile of a drug abuser. Have students think about someone they know who abuses drugs. The person can be a peer or an adult. Think of the length of time this person has used drugs, what drugs are used, when they are used, the person's positive qualities and his or her weaknesses.

Have each student express a unique characteristic of the person he or she is thinking about. Be sure to suggest positive characteristics as well as negative ones. Ask:

● What are some of the patterns you see revealed by what you have identified?

● What problems are revealed?

● What are some of the different reasons people take drugs?

● What would a society in which no drugs were used be like?

6. Personal values and decision-making related to drug use. Ask:

● What are your feelings about common, daily use

of stimulants and depressants?

● How do your parents feel about drug use?

● Is one drug more serious than another? Why?

● What have your parents said to you about using drugs?

● Why might you choose not to use drugs, even though your parents may use them, or approve of your using them?

● What is a drug problem?

● How might a teenager's drug misuse affect his or her family? How does a parent's drug abuse affect teenagers?

7. Learning how to say no. Say: "Before you can help another with a drug problem, you must know how you stand on this issue. What are your values about drug use? What do you do when you are pressured to become involved?

"Pretend that you arrive at a party where nearly everyone is drinking. You are offered a drink. You say you don't want one. Although they don't tease you outright, you can tell the others are suspicious of you. They keep their distance. A few make cutting statements to you. What can you say?"

Ask someone to take the role of the person wanting to refuse. The other group members are people at the party. After this activity, ask:

● How did you feel when everyone pressured you?

● How can you stand up for your values and decisions?

● Would others in this group find it hard to say no? Why or why not?

● What are some effective ways to deal with a situation like this?

8. Practice talking to a friend with a drug problem. Have students think of a friend they know or have known who has a drug problem. If anyone does not know such a person, suggest he or she use the profile developed by the group earlier.

Divide the group into pairs. Have each partner take a turn at being the friend with the problem and the other partner being a peer minister to this friend. After 15 to 20 minutes bring the group together.

RESPONSE

Use the following questions for debriefing this activity and helping students respond to what they have experienced. Questions under the "Necessary transition questions" section should always be asked. The points you want to emphasize are summarized following the questions.

9. Necessary transition questions:
- As a peer minister, what skills seemed successful?
- What skills need improvement?
- As a counselee, how did the peer minister help you?
- What skills seemed most effective?

10. Examining the experience:
- How effective do you feel the counseling session was?
- What do you think your friend would really do if he or she were approached in this manner?
- What may be a deeper problem in your friend's life than the drug problem? What might be the cause of this problem?
- Have you ever discussed this problem with your friend? Why or why not?

11. Points to make about the learning activity:
- Often a drug problem cannot be resolved until deeper problems such as low self-esteem, boredom or loneliness are addressed.
- The most important task of a peer minister in helping someone with a drug problem is to lead the person to professional help. Peer ministers can be

"bridges" between troubled students and professionals.

● Peer ministers cannot take over and do the work for troubled students. Counselees must make the actual contact themselves when seeking help from adults.

● Peer ministers can't "save" anyone. Not all people want to be helped. Even if a peer minister has done all he or she can, the troubled student still has the choice to harbor the problem.

● Drug abuse problems often take a long time to overcome. Discouragement may hit peer ministers while trying to help. It is important to keep trying.

● Explore how to deal with the causes of drug abuse such as pressure, fear and boredom. Suggest to peer ministers that they bring counselees into the youth group. Peer ministers need to remember they have power to intervene and prevent drug use by reaching out to other kids through Christian love and concern. Ministry within a youth group can provide genuine highs that take the place of cheap ones.

CLOSING

12. Ask for the Observer's report. Allow time for individuals to react to the observations.

13. Friendship: the highest of highs. Help students see that a benefit of peer ministry training is cultivating friendship. The benefits of friendship far exceed those that substances offer.

Say that a substance abuser's biggest problem is not the substance. The hang-ups and self-defeating behaviors were there before the abuse problem, and will still be there when the abuser chooses to stop.

Tell students that often we don't see ourselves as God's creations—but we are. We deny that our bodies are temples of God—but they are. Peer ministers can help substance abusers by letting them know their value as God's creations—and then getting them to professional counseling.

As a group, do a communion service. Stress that the substances used in communion symbolize something much greater than simple bread and wine. They represent the body of Christ, and the group's communion as friends.

*H*OMEWORK ASSIGNMENT . . .

Although it will be difficult for them, ask students to initiate a conversation with a substance-abusing friend. Students should express concern and a willingness to help the friend get professional assistance. Find out where drug counseling is available in the school and community.

HANDOUT:

Anonymous Quiz

Place a checkmark in the "Yes" or "No" box as the statements apply to you. Do not sign your name.

	Yes	No
I have never tasted an alcoholic drink.	☐	☐
I have never been drunk.	☐	☐
I have had a drink in the past two weeks.	☐	☐
I easily could get marijuana.	☐	☐
I have tried hallucinogens.	☐	☐
Some of my close friends have tried hallucinogens.	☐	☐
I have spiked my dog's water dish.	☐	☐
I have persuaded someone else to drink alcohol.	☐	☐
I have successfully discouraged someone else from drinking or taking drugs.	☐	☐
I think marijuana should be legalized.	☐	☐
My parents drink quite often.	☐	☐
The decision to use or abuse drugs or alcohol is up to the individual.	☐	☐
What may be right for some may not be right for others.	☐	☐
Christians should not hang around substance abusers.	☐	☐
I think some members of our youth group have a problem with drinking.	☐	☐
Some people in our youth group abuse drugs.	☐	☐
I once vowed never to drink, but have since broken that promise.	☐	☐
The legal age for drinking should be lowered.	☐	☐
Penalties for drunken driving should be more strict.	☐	☐
Alcohol should be banned in our community.	☐	☐
Substance use is okay as long as it is done in moderation.	☐	☐

Relationships With the Opposite Sex

SESSION OBJECTIVES

Students will:

1. Examine their values on sexuality, dating and marriage.

2. Practice peer ministry for helping those with problems with relating to the opposite sex.

SCRIPTURE FOUNDATION

And They Will Become One Flesh

The Lord God took the man and put him in the Garden of Eden to work it and take care of it. And the Lord God commanded the man, "You are free to eat from any tree in the garden; but you must not eat from the tree of the knowledge of good and evil, for when you eat of it you will surely die."

The Lord God said, "It is not good for the man to be alone. I will make a helper suitable for him."

So the Lord God caused the man to fall into a deep sleep; and while he was sleeping, he took one of the man's ribs and closed up the place with flesh. Then the Lord God made a woman from the rib he had taken out of the man, and he brought her to the man.

The man said, "This is now bone of my bones and flesh of my flesh; she shall be called 'woman,' for she was taken out of man." For this reason a man will

*leave his father and mother and be united to his
wife, and they will become one flesh.*
    *The man and his wife were both naked, and they
felt no shame.*
—Genesis 2:15-18, 21-25

Christian beliefs about sexuality and male-female
relationships have varied widely from place to place
and time to time. Since the beginning, however, men
and women have sensed that although they are whole
and complete without the other, they are powerfully
driven toward each other. Lewis B. Smedes, in *Sex
for Christians* (Wm. B. Eerdmans), tells how men and
women find communion in their sexuality:

> *"Eve was not Adam's 'better half'—nor is any
> woman a man's half. Male and female are in move-
> ment toward each other and yet away from each
> other, each needing the other to be himself/herself, yet
> each needing to be an individual in his/her own
> right.*
>   *". . . Biblical revelation tells us to stop thinking of
> ourselves as isolated islands of rational God-likeness
> and think of ourselves instead as coming into real
> humanity when we live in genuine personal fellow-
> ship with others."*

We read in Matthew 19 how the Pharisees had
taken most of the joy and mystery out of sexuality,
reducing it to a corpus of rules. After Jesus affirmed
the scripture given from Genesis, the Pharisees asked,
"Why then did Moses command that a man give his
wife a certificate of divorce and send her away?"
    Jesus pointed out that Moses gave the law because
the people were irresponsible and selfish: " . . . your
hearts were hard. But it was not this way from the
beginning."
    Matthew 19:12 surfaces yet another real issue for
young people today: Should they get married or stay

single? In this verse the Lord points out that some are able to live as single while others can't. The verse indicates some stay single for the sake of the kingdom of heaven. This is true for some people, but others remain single only to avoid dealing with divorce in the future.

This issue leads to the question of morality, which seems almost an unknown concept to modern youth. The scriptures forbid sexual relations outside of marriage. And as with all things, the Lord has our best interest in mind when he prohibits this. Sexual immorality deliberately uses another person to gratify an entirely selfish desire. In contrast, God requires that the one-flesh union be reserved for marriage—the lifelong partnership of self-giving love. Those who commit sexual immorality seek to avoid this commitment and simply take advantage of the "partner."

Young people may not want to hear these things or deal with them. But it is critical to have students deal with the significance of Christian principles and behavior as opposed to non-Christian values. If research on Christian teenagers' sexual behaviors is correct, they aren't acting all that much differently from non-Christian kids.

*P*REPARATION

1. Prepare the meeting area for the training group: warm, comfortable and not too large or too small. Obtain a chalkboard or newsprint pad. Photocopy a "For Guys Only" handout for each guy and a "For Girls Only" handout for each girl.

2. Read carefully through the session, becoming fully prepared and aware of its objectives and learning activities.

3. To help you think through the purpose and direction of this session, answer the following questions

either in writing or in thought:
- What is my Christian understanding of dating?
- What is my Christian understanding of sexuality?
- What is my understanding of sexual behavior from a Christian orientation?
- In what ways does this understanding limit my life? In what ways does it expand my life?
- What do I believe about the stewardship of my body?
- How can I witness to others in the area of sexuality?
- What additional questions, points or examples can I use in making this lesson meaningful?
- Additional notes to myself:

4. This topic touches sensitive areas in the lives of all your students. It involves personal values, parental values and behaviors, and ethical considerations.

Parents rightfully reserve the responsibility and privilege to teach their children about sexuality. Some parents resent the intrusion of others. Show your respect for parental ideals.

Often students begin this discussion with laughter and nervousness. From the moment you start the session, express seriousness and respect for this subject. As you set the tone for the discussion, students will respond in kind.

Peer Ministry Training

OPENING

1. Pray. Open with a prayer by asking for God's guidance as participants seek to serve him.

2. Assign an Observer; and ask for homework reports.

3. Complete the "For Guys Only" and "For Girls Only" handouts. After all are finished with the worksheets, ask the group to look over the responses. What are some common reactions? If possible, average the group's responses to each item.

SKILLS DEVELOPMENT

4. Relationship to the opposite sex. Gather everyone and ask:

● What opportunities do you have to meet friends of the opposite sex?

● What do you talk about when you are with someone of the opposite sex? Why do you sometimes feel uncomfortable in these situations?

● What does it mean to have a boyfriend or girlfriend?

● Is it important in your school to have one? Why or why not?

● What are you expected to do with a boyfriend or girlfriend?

● Can you be a friend without being a boyfriend or girlfriend? What is the difference?

● Have volunteers read aloud Mark 14:3-9; Romans 16:1-2; 1 Corinthians 6:18-19; Galatians 5:22-23; and Titus 2:6-7. After the reading of each passage, ask the group to list the relationship qualities in it.

5. Discussing situations. Ask the group members what they think is the most critical problem for teenagers in the area of sexuality. Encourage all members of the group to share.

Then choose one or more of the following situations and as a group talk about the long-term consequences of the problem. Then discuss how students would counsel the person involved in the situation.

● An attractive person of the opposite sex invites you to watch television alone at his or her house.

● Several peers invite you to watch an X-rated video this Friday night.

● A good friend thinks she is pregnant and considers abortion.

● A friend believes he or she is unattractive.

● Your best friend had sex for the first time last week.

● A peer freezes at the thought of asking someone out for a date.

● A peer confides in you that he or she has homosexual desires.

● A person in your youth group trusts you with the secret that she has been repeatedly sexually abused by her father.

RESPONSE

Use the following questions for debriefing this activity and helping students respond to what they have experienced. Questions under the "Necessary transition questions" section should always be asked. The points you want to emphasize are summarized following the questions.

6. Necessary transition questions:

● What have you learned that will help you counsel a person in one of these situations?

● How can you help your friends who struggle with these issues?

● What are the critical issues you need to face in your current behavior and relationships that will ensure personal joy and satisfaction in future intimate relationships?

● What are the important qualities you look for in someone you might want to marry?

7. Examining the experience:

● How do you decide your standards for sexual behavior?

● How can you deal constructively with sexual approaches that don't meet your standards?

● What do young people do to invite sexual advances? Why might they do this?

● Who carries the major responsibility in a couple for determining sexual behavior? Why?

● What do you feel about homosexuality?

● Where can you get information about unwanted pregnancies, venereal diseases and AIDS?

8. Points to make about the learning activity:

● Sexual behavior affects the development of your personal life and your relationship to others. Although often treated lightly, it can be a great source of happiness or unhappiness in your personal life.

● Self-confidence is always a critical issue in relationships, whether for those who desire warm, loving relationships or for those who feel they need to engage in sexual intercourse to prove themselves.

● It is vital to decide your standards before engaging in close relationships. Emotions, which are natural and easily aroused, can distort your judgment if you haven't previously decided on specific standards.

● Peer influence can have a powerful effect on the general standards of male-female relationships.

● Research has shown that premarital sex negatively affects sex within marriage.

● There is more to marriage than sex.

● Discussing sex is good and healthy, and putting

it into a proper perspective leads to a normal and beautiful aspect of human relationships.

CLOSING

9. Ask for the Observer's report. Allow time for individuals to react to the observations.

10. Male and female he created them. Have students affirm God's creation of male and female. Ask them to complete these statements: "I am thankful God created men because . . ." and "I am thankful God created women because . . ." List the responses verbatim on the board or newsprint.

After all have contributed, review the list. Chances are good that the comments will have concentrated on intimacy and friendship. Point out that those qualities also are qualities of peer ministry, and that one day the skills they learn as friends will be invaluable in marriage. Then read the following from *Sex, Love, or Infatuation* by Ray E. Short (Augsburg):

> *"One of the great privileges of marriage is to have children . . .*
>
> *"What a sacred trust! What a joy when that tiny babe comes as a gift from God, with the full blessing of society and loved ones.*
>
> *"But how sobering to think that those two little eyes never would have opened if you two had not known intimacy. Those tiny fingers and hands would never have touched if you had not shared with each other . . .*
>
> *"In its fullest meaning, sex is a sacred ritual through which two human personalities are joined in every part of their being."*

Stand in a circle with arms around shoulders. Pray: "God, thank you for the gift of sexuality. Help us to see your gift as you created it—help us see the world's view of sex as harmful to us and others. In Jesus' name, amen."

HOMEWORK ASSIGNMENT . . .

Ask the students to talk with a peer of the opposite sex (but not a boyfriend or girlfriend) about the qualities they like to see in guys or girls. Also have students ask the peer what turns him or her off.

HANDOUTS:

For Guys Only

Rate each of the following traits the way you'd like to see them in girls (1 = hate to see this in girls; 5 = I'm not sure; 10 = I like to see this in girls).

1. Lots of makeup   1 2 3 4 5 6 7 8 9 10

2. Looks like she stepped from a fashion catalog   1 2 3 4 5 6 7 8 9 10

3. Gentle spirit   1 2 3 4 5 6 7 8 9 10

4. Sexy body   1 2 3 4 5 6 7 8 9 10

5. Loving   1 2 3 4 5 6 7 8 9 10

6. Makes all the guys drool   1 2 3 4 5 6 7 8 9 10

7. Takes life seriously   1 2 3 4 5 6 7 8 9 10

8. Spits tobacco   1 2 3 4 5 6 7 8 9 10

9. Acts cold and uncaring   1 2 3 4 5 6 7 8 9 10

10. Sensitive   1 2 3 4 5 6 7 8 9 10

11. Cuts other people down with her sarcastic wit   1 2 3 4 5 6 7 8 9 10

12. Swears a lot   1 2 3 4 5 6 7 8 9 10

For Girls Only

Rate each of the following traits the way you'd like to see them in guys (1 = I hate to see this in guys; 5 = I'm not sure; 10 = I like to see this in guys).

1. Tough, macho   1 2 3 4 5 6 7 8 9 10

2. Cuts other people down with his
    sarcastic wit   1 2 3 4 5 6 7 8 9 10

3. Swears a lot   1 2 3 4 5 6 7 8 9 10

4. Spits tobacco   1 2 3 4 5 6 7 8 9 10

5. Meek   1 2 3 4 5 6 7 8 9 10

6. Has a sense of humor   1 2 3 4 5 6 7 8 9 10

7. Drives a fast car   1 2 3 4 5 6 7 8 9 10

8. Drinks   1 2 3 4 5 6 7 8 9 10

9. Wears great clothes   1 2 3 4 5 6 7 8 9 10

10. Takes life seriously   1 2 3 4 5 6 7 8 9 10

11. Loving   1 2 3 4 5 6 7 8 9 10

12. Sensitive   1 2 3 4 5 6 7 8 9 10

Death, Dying and Suicide

SESSION OBJECTIVES

Students will:

1. Learn to comfort someone who has experienced the death of a loved one.

2. Learn to talk with a dying person (optional).

3. Learn to talk with someone contemplating suicide (optional).

SCRIPTURE FOUNDATION

I Am the Resurrection and the Life

On his arrival, Jesus found that Lazarus had already been in the tomb for four days. Bethany was less than two miles from Jerusalem, and many Jews had come to Martha and Mary to comfort them in the loss of their brother. When Martha heard that Jesus was coming, she went out to meet him, but Mary stayed at home.

"Lord," Martha said to Jesus, "if you had been here, my brother would not have died. But I know that even now God will give you whatever you ask."

Jesus said to her, "Your brother will rise again."

Martha answered, "I know he will rise again in the resurrection at the last day."

Jesus said to her, "I am the resurrection and the life. He who believes in me will live, even though he dies; and whoever lives and believes in me will never die. Do you believe this?"

"Yes, Lord," she told him, "I believe that you are the Christ, the Son of God, who was to come into the world."

—*John 11:17-27*

In talking to Martha about Lazarus' death, Jesus makes the powerful affirmation, "I am the resurrection and the life." Christ speaks of life on two levels: the eternal life beyond physical death we all must face; and the day-to-day living in God's grace and purposes. Christ has overcome death and put it in proper perspective, but he also fills our present earthly life with significance. Only through faith in Christ can a human truly know comfort and freedom from fear when facing death.

When sorrow comes, life is bewildering and the heart aches. It is possible to read comforting books about life and heaven and immortality, even the Bible, and still receive little comfort. At such times a friend can come, and with a few words, bring the comfort the heart craves. Friends can do what print cannot do. God sends more comfort through people than through any other means. This is why it's important to have the courage and skill to be God's messengers of comfort.

"Praise be to the God and Father of our Lord Jesus Christ, the Father of compassion and the God of all comfort, who comforts us in all our troubles, so that we can comfort those in any trouble with the comfort we ourselves have received from God" (2 Corinthians 1:3-4). As God comforts us, we are equipped to comfort others. By experiencing God's comfort, we can pass on what we have received. Jesus said, "Blessed are those who mourn, for they shall be comforted" (Matthew 5:4). We can be his instruments of comfort.

PREPARATION

1. Prepare the meeting area for the training group: warm, comfortable and not too large or too small. Obtain a chalkboard or newsprint pad.

2. Read carefully through the session, becoming fully prepared and aware of its objectives and learning activities.

3. To help you think through the purpose and direction of this session, answer the following questions either in writing or in thought:

● How do my beliefs about death influence the way I live?

● What can be the negative effects on my life if I dwell on death?

● Why might a Christian be unable to comfort another at the time of a death?

● If a pastor is asked to conduct a funeral of a non-Christian, how should he or she respond?

● What does it mean to me to live daily in God's grace and purpose?

● What additional questions, points or examples can I use in making this lesson meaningful?

● Additional notes to myself:

4. The topic of death often leads to sharing personal beliefs as well as fears. Likewise, it is an area where the peer minister may feel more uncomfortable than the person being helped. Feeling comfortable about the topic of death is the prime focus of this session.

It is possible that some students in your group have not been close to death. If so, they can be brought into the session by including the loss of a friend through a move, rejection or changing lifestyles.

5. This session's primary focus is on being there for peers who experience grief in the loss of a loved one. Optional material has been included for helping the terminally ill and those contemplating suicide. You probably will not have time to cover all three topics. Choose the topic that most fits your group's concerns.

Peer Ministry Training

OPENING

1. Pray. Open with a prayer by asking for God's guidance as participants seek to serve him.

2. Assign an Observer; and ask for homework reports.

3. Introduce the topic of death. Ask:

● How many of you have experienced the death of someone close to you?

● What were some of your emotions and thoughts?

● What helped you get through this period?

● What did your friends do or not do to help?

● Why is it hard for us to talk to another about the death of a loved one?

Ask the following questions about the death of a friendship:

● How many of you have experienced the death of a friendship?

● How many of you have had a close friend move to another city or state?

- What were some of your emotions at that time?
- What helped you get through this period?
- Were your parents or other friends aware of what you were going through? Why or why not?
- Why might it be hard to talk to another about such a loss?

SKILLS DEVELOPMENT

4. Discussion of comfort and help. Ask the following questions relating to different aspects of death.

Understanding death:
- What does death mean to you?
- What has your family discussed about death?
- Who has brought up the subject?
- What are your fears about death?
- What has led you to have these fears?

Rituals surrounding death:
- What are some of the rituals that surround death?
- What are the purposes of these rituals?
- How are they comforting? How might they make death more difficult?
- Who often is the first to reach out and comfort the bereaved family? a pastor? neighbor? close friend?
- How might faith help at a time like this?
- How could you help a friend who has lost a loved one?

Terminal illness (optional):
- Why would it be difficult to talk to someone with a terminal illness?
- What emotions or fears could block communication between you and the terminally ill person?
- How would it help the terminally ill person if you were to talk to him or her?

Suicide (optional):
- How might a family react to a suicide in comparison with a death from natural causes?

● What are some of the reasons people commit suicide?

● How could a suicide be prevented?

● What clues should you look for in a potential suicide? (Some signs of suicidal thoughts include giving away precious possessions; *any* mention or plan of a suicide; dramatic changes in behavior; previous suicide attempts; drug abuse; unstable personality; and little interaction with others.)

● What effect might the following statement have on a potential suicide victim: "I don't want you to kill yourself"?

● How could you communicate with a friend to keep him or her from committing suicide?

● How could a group help someone who is considering suicide? who has lost a loved one?

5. Practicing skills in dealing with death. A person in the group may be dealing with the death of a loved one. If so, ask this person if he or she would like to talk about it with the group. When finished, let individuals in the group respond to him or her. You will need to take the initiative in this.

If no one is dealing with the death of a loved one, ask for two volunteers to role work in front of the group. One student has lost a loved one; the other is the peer minister.

After debriefing this with the group, divide into pairs and have partners practice each role. It is important that everyone in the group experience what it is like to express comforting words. Some have never done this before.

6. Talking to a terminally ill person (optional). Follow the same procedure as in step 5, except change the focus to a terminally ill person.

7. Talking to someone contemplating suicide (optional). Follow the same procedure as in step 5, except change the focus to a suicidal person. Review with the group the following points before role working:

● The person contemplating suicide makes contact for a reason: He or she needs help.

● Often the person does not want to kill himself or herself.

● The expression of emotion makes him or her less likely to commit suicide; for every minute a person uses to communicate anguish and fear, he or she moves further away from a suicide.

● You should never be falsely positive by ignoring or denying the indications of depression.

● Abstract speeches about your personal feelings of life and death will not help.

● You must allow the person to explore his or her feelings and to deal with depression or anguish.

RESPONSE

Use the following questions for debriefing this activity and helping students respond to what they have experienced. Questions under the "Necessary transition questions" section should always be asked. The points you want to emphasize are summarized following the questions.

8. Necessary transition questions:

● How well did the peer minister deal with the issue of death?

● How comfortable did the counselee feel about talking about death?

● Why is it so hard to talk about the death of someone we love?

9. Examining the experience:

● Have you experienced the death of someone close to you? If so, describe what the experience did to you.

● What helps people get through grieving? terminal illness? suicidal thoughts?

● How does your view of death influence the way you live?

● What is "eternal life" and what does it mean *now?*

10. Points to make about the learning activity:

● Rituals such as funerals serve many emotional and psychological purposes. They provide strength and comfort in the sharing of faith and the gathering of friends. They provide activities during the initial shock period. They help loved ones accept the reality of the death. Some say one needs to see a loved one's body to make a final departure from that person.

● Much attention is given to loved ones at the time of the death and funeral. Often, however, the bereaved are neglected in the following weeks when the reality of death and subsequent sorrow and perhaps depression are the strongest. This is when a friend or peer minister is truly needed.

● Our personal fears and feelings of inadequacy often stifle us from speaking to a bereaved person. It is normal to feel inadequate. We cannot bring back the life of the loved one. But we can express our sorrow and *be there* for the hurting person.

● Letting people express their emotions and sorrow shows you are listening to them. You don't need to give "solutions" or ideas. This is a time when your skill in asking open-ended, feeling-level questions is needed.

● If you truly care about others, you will be there with them in their grief. When you care, the caring comes through irrespective of the inadequacy of the words.

● While talking with a terminally ill person, be aware of his or her emotions toward the impending death. Is he or she denying it? accepting it? angry? depressed? The least helpful words you can say are speculations of why God allows things like this. Don't be a "friend" like Job's "friends."

● Talking with someone contemplating suicide can be confusing; he or she will probably present a "surface" problem. That's why you must know the cries for help from someone thinking about suicide.

● Never deny a person's feelings of depression or fear. Let the peer explore his or her feelings.

● Always refer a peer contemplating suicide to a professional counselor or pastor. This is a crisis situation—you need to take the person by the hand to a professional.

Closing

11. Ask for the Observer's report. Allow time for individuals to react to the observations.

12. Peer ministry commissioning. Use the Closing from Session 8.

Homework assignment . . .

Ask students to talk with their parents about deaths that have occurred in the family. Tell the students to ask how the parents' faith (or lack of it) affected them in their grief. Ask the parents about their view of the Resurrection and how it affects the way they live today.

Dynamic Resources for Your Ministry

▶ Determining Needs in Your Youth Ministry
by Dr. Peter L. Benson and Dorothy L. Williams
foreword by George Gallup, Jr.

Identify and respond to the specific needs and concerns of your young people. **Determining Needs In Your Youth Ministry** helps you get honest answers to important questions. You'll zero in on the needs of any group of young people. Youth group. Sunday school class. Youth choir, and more.

This handy do-it-yourself research kit helps you uncover the real issues facing your young people. The complete kit includes . . .

- 20 ready-to-use questionnaires and answer sheets
- Tally and summary sheets
- Detailed "how-to-use" information
- Interpretation guidelines
- Practical programming suggestions for using survey results

Open new, positive lines of communication with your kids. And plan programs that really meet their needs with this professional ministry tool.

ISBN 0931-529-56-5, $19.95

▶ Friend to Friend
by J. David Stone and Larry Keefauver

Learn a simple yet powerful method for helping a friend sort through a tough situation. The friend-to-friend process is a non-professional counseling approach anyone can use to help a friend through a problem.

Use it in your own ministry with kids. Or teach your young people how to minister effectively to others, friend to friend.

ISBN 0936-664-11-8, $5.95

▶ Youth Ministry Care Cards

Keep in touch with your group members—with **Youth Ministry Care Cards**. They're a quick, low-cost way to build attendance and give affirmation. **Youth Ministry Care Cards** are inspiring, attention-grabbing post cards your kids will love to get. Each card includes a meaningful Bible verse, a colorful cartoon and a place for a brief personal message.

Affirmations—encouraging messages to let kids know you're thinking about them.

Attendance Builders—unforgettable reminders to attract more kids to your meetings, retreats and special events.

Keep a supply on hand so you can jot a quick note of affirmation right when you think of it. You get 6 colorful designs in each 30-card packet. Get a dozen different messages when you order both packets.

Affirmations
ISBN 0931-529-28-X, $3.95/pack

Attendance Builders
ISBN 0931-529-36-0, $3.95/pack

▶ *Student Plan-It Calendar*
by Lee Sparks and Cindy Hansen

Help active teenagers stay focused on Christ as they coordinate their busy lives. This nifty organizer puts kids in charge of their time.

The **Student Plan-It Calendar** is a colorful, easy-to-tote devotional calendar that helps teenagers keep track of their busy schedules during the school year—and summer!

It's appealing. Fun to use. And it has a place for everything . . .

- Work and class schedules
- Addresses and phone numbers
- Appointments
- Important reminders
- Assignments
- Special dates

Plus, scores of inspiring quotations and weekly devotional activities help young people stay focused on Christian attitudes and actions. Give those special teenagers in your life the **Student Plan-It Calendar** for graduation or as a going-back-to-school gift.

Student Plan-It Calendar, $5.95

▶ *Controversial Topics for Youth Groups*
by Edward N. McNulty

Get essential tools for teaching young people how to deal with tough issues. Help teenagers develop the skills they'll need to make ethical decisions. Plus, get 40 creative program ideas for examining thought-provoking topics, such as . . .

- Reincarnation
- AIDS: Punishment for immorality?
- Loyalty to a friend who cheats
- Christians and politics
- Abortion, and 35 other hot topics

Teach your young people how to think through hard issues, apply scriptural values, then make their own faith-based decisions.

You'll get loads of current background information. Ready-to-use program ideas. Plus, dozens of creative approaches for handling life's hot topics.

ISBN 0931-529-51-4, $13.95